A CASE OF

Vintage Claret

*Fifty of the best
Burnley footballers
of all-time*

James Crabtree, Burnley and England full back, 1882-95.

Crabtree was an outstanding defender who made a great reputation for himself on the international scene and was equally comfortable playing either at full or half back.

A CASE OF

Vintage Claret

*Fifty of the best
Burnley footballers
of all-time*

David Wiseman

*To Michael
With every good wish
David Wiseman*

Hudson and Pearson

Published by Hudson & Pearson Ltd. 2006

10 9 8 7 6 5 4 3 2 1

Copyright © David Wiseman

David Wiseman has asserted his right under the
Copyright, Designs and Patents Act 1988 to be identified
as the author of this work

First published in Great Britain in 2006 by
Hudson & Pearson Ltd.

Hudson & Pearson Ltd.
Bradwood Works, Manchester Road, Dunnockshaw,
Burnley, Lancashire BB11 5PW

A CIP catalogue record for this book
is available from the British Library

ISBN 13 No. 978-0-9554017-0-1
ISBN 10 No. 0-9554017-0-4

Typeset by Hudson & Pearson Ltd.
in 11pt Palatino

Printed and bound in Great Britain
by Hudson & Pearson Ltd., Dunnockshaw, Burnley, Lancashire

Foreword

What follows here is my very personal selection as to who have been some of the best "Clarets" in the history of Burnley Football Club. (I put "Clarets" in inverted commas, because some of them played pre-1911, when the club wore green and a variety of other colours!)

This choice is purely personal – you may and will have other ideas! On reflection, the only two things that all the players mentioned here have in common, is that at one time or another: one, they all played for Burnley; and, secondly, they were all seen by one or other of four generations of the Wiseman family! I never saw any of the pre-war Clarets play, but my grandad and my dad did. And before I learned to walk and talk, I was listening to their memories. Because of this, I was a "CLARET" before I ever went to Turf Moor in 1946!

But the major problem in compiling this list of "all time greats" was not who to include, but who to leave out! Even now, having made my selection, I could have thought of quite a few others.

For instance, what about Scottish International Jock Aird, a more than decent right back in the early 1950's, or his Scottish partner, Doug Winton (both at Jeanfield Swifts and Turf Moor). Between them, they played well over 300 times for the club. Did I leave Doug Winton out because he once missed a penalty against New Brighton, when we won 9-0? The only time in my lifetime that we might have scored ten at the Turf, and he missed a penalty! Unforgivable!

Tom Bamford, another fine right back was in the 1914 Cup winning team, whilst Alf Bassnett was a defender to reckon with in the 1920's. Bamford and Bassnett both played 157 games for the first team. How our club could do with the likes of Ian Brennan (1970's) these days. He topped 200 games and is still remembered for the goal he scored for Burnley at Anfield. And whilst talking of goals, what about the winner against Orient, scored by Ian Britton? Sorry, no place for Ian. Even though without that goal, there might have been no club to write about! Couldn't find space either for Britton's two Orient colleagues, Neil Grewcock and Ray Deakin (captain that day).

Harry Thomson, 1959-69
"A God in a green jersey" – surely, worthy of inclusion!

Still on goalscorers, what about Victorians Tom Nicol or Walter Place (junior). No place here for that Place there! Or Dick Smith (76 goals), the first goal scoring hero of the 20th Century at Turf Moor. A host of 1920's and 1930's heroes failed to make the cut – Walter Weaver, John Steel, Gilbert Richmond, and "big" Cecil Smith.

Irish Internationals Tommy Cassidy, Terry Cochrane and Sammy Todd are all omitted, fifties stalwart, Albert Cheesebrough misses out and so do his colleagues, right wingers Billy Gray and Doug Newlands, both tricky, fast and partners of Jimmy "Mac", Even a few from the great days of the 1960's don't quite manage to make these pages – Walter Joyce, "big" John Talbut, and Harry Thomson ("A God in a green jersey!")

Not everyone from the 1970's gets in my selection either. Sadly, no room for Mick Docherty or Ray Hankin (46 goals) or utility man Geoff Nulty, Or even the memorable and entertaining Tommy Hutchinson.

No space either for several in the 1980's. Kevin Hird, (only two seasons, but 31 goals from midfield!) full back Brian Laws, left winger Joe Jakub (70's, 80's and 90's!), or even Tony Morley, (who went on to win most things in football with Aston Villa!). Steve Taylor (52 goals), Steve Davis (the Barnsley one!), dancing Chris Pearce (248 games) and Kevin Young (early 80's) all just failed to make it.

Indeed, I admit to leaving out far more than I have included! There have been a lot of players at Turf Moor over the years, stretching from A to Z. Or in Turf Moor terms, from Abbott to Zelem! However, please read, remember and enjoy, whether you agree or disagree!

Rev. David Wiseman
July 2006, Skipton

P.S. And what about Billy Dougall and Ray Bennion (they didn't play too much, but their contribution as trainers, coaches, etc was the greatest in the history of the club. From Tommy Lawton to Jimmy McIlroy, they all owe a debt to this pair). And have you forgotten Bob "The Toff" Brocklebank (pre war) or his partner Billy "Golden" Miller, one of the finest ball players of all. And we haven't even mentioned Dave Merrington, Peter Kippax or Peter O'Dowd. But just wait and see who I have included!.

PPS. There is a tradition of drinking Benedictine liquer in many Burnley public houses. It is an old and proud tradition. If there is a similar thirst for some more vintage claret amongst the folks in town, there might be another case on its way!

PPPS What follows are not complete "life stories". I have concentrated on playing careers whilst at Burnley – what we saw, and remember, whilst they were "Clarets".

Dedication

To the four generations of the Wiseman family, who for over a century, saw and remembered all of the players included in this book. My grandad Joseph Wiseman, my dad George Wiseman, my son Christian Wiseman, and myself (making up the number!)

Acknowledgements

Since I first wrote my history of Burnley Football Club *Up the Clarets* (1973) and the illustrated history *Vintage Claret* (1975), there have been many fine books written about Burnley, its football club and its history. To supplement my own experience, I have dipped into numerous other Claret compilations, especially *Burnley; A Complete Record* by Edward Lee and Ray Simpson and *The Clarets Collection* by Ray Simpson. I wish to acknowledge my appreciation of the work they have put into their research which has helped me and others no end.

Also *Football League Players Records 1946-2005* by Barry Hugman and *Football League Players Records 1888-1939* by Michael Joyce. Both are monumental works which can only draw words of praise and appreciation from other football historians such as me.

Once again, as I did in 1973, I must acknowledge the help from those days of Burnley librarians Richard Caul and Ross Burton. Much of the material I gleaned in the 1970's has been reused in a different format 35 years later. And I must also acknowledge the great help of Edward Lee at the *Burnley Express* for his help in collating the photographs. And finally, as much as any other source of information, my thanks go to generations of football reporters of the local press (from "Kestrel" via Don Smith to Keith McNee), whose work I have quoted because they were there at the time, and so their memory didn't play any tricks. They wrote what they saw!

Contents

Jimmy Adamson, Footballer Of The Year, 1961-62

Jimmy ADAMSON

1947-64

Half back
426 league games
17 goals

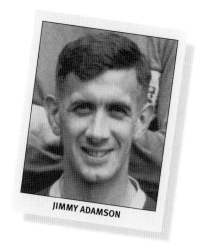

JIMMY ADAMSON

Jimmy Adamson was a multi talented person – player, coach, manager – those are just a few of his many roles. But it is as a skilled half back and a born leader of men that I remember him the best. Jimmy was one of the earlier products of the North East conveyor belt of talent that produced such a steady supply of first team material in the 50's and 60's.

Jimmy Adamson played in a variety of positions after his arrival at Turf Moor in 1947. That was probably the reason why it was another three seasons before he won his way into the first team. The date was 6 February 1950 and the place was Burnden Park in Bolton. The Burnley team that day read: Strong; Aird, Mather; Adamson, Cummings, Bray; Chew, Morris, Holden, McIlroy, Hays.

That day, Jimmy was filling in for the injured Reg Attwell the established right half back, but such was the maturity and confidence of the young debutant, that when Reg returned, he rarely occupied the right half position again. That was the start of Jimmy Adamson's remarkable career at Burnley.

In the next 12 seasons, he only missed a handful of games, all due to injury. Half-backs came in my mind in threes, and every team worthy of the name had a fine half back line in the middle of the field. They were the engine room that ran the team. I was brought up on "Attwell, Brown and Bray", but for me, they were surpassed by "Adamson, Cummings and Shannon" (and later Shannon was replaced by Brian Miller). Let's examine the structure a little closer.

All the top teams had much the same format – a strong centre half, a classy skilful half back and a hard tackling, robust half back. So it was, Portsmouth had Scoular, Froggatt and Dickinson, Wolves had Clamp, Slater, and Flowers; Spurs had Blanchflower, Norman and McKay, and Burnley had Adamson, Cummings and Miller. Adamson was Burnley's "Blanchflower" – the genius of the defence and the player who controlled the midfield.

Jimmy Adamson always stood out on any field; his height of course helped, but it was his style of play, his strong tackling and his superb distribution skills that more than caught the eye. I can picture him now, breaking out of defence and spraying passes across the field, but particularly in the direction of his great colleague, Jimmy McIlroy. Sooner or later he had to be recognised by the selectors, and in March 1953, he was chosen to represent England "B". It is interesting to note that Jimmy was comfortable in all three half back positions, and over his time in the first team, he had long spells, on the right, on the left and in the centre.

The Adamson-McIlroy partnership grew in fame until it was recognised as among the best on every field in the country, and beyond. By now, "Mac" was an established International and it soon became a popular saying that "Jimmy Adamson was the best uncapped player in England!"

He never was fully recognised by his country, though in his time he played for the Football League as well as England "B". But it was also his captaincy for which I remember Jimmy Adamson. His leadership and his coolness under pressure were his keynotes, and alongside Tommy Boyle and Alan Brown, he must rank as one of the best club captains ever at Turf Moor.

He led the Clarets throughout the fifties, and he captained them in their League Championship season of 1959-60. (It was a typical Adamson season – he was an ever present, playing 15 times at right half, three times at centre half, and 32 games at left half) He led them in Europe in 1960-61, and he took the club to within two games of achieving the League and Cup double in 1961-62. With only a decent run of luck, Adamson and Burnley would be remembered to this day across the land, as the captain and the club which achieved the "impossible". As it was, after setting the pace all season, the club only won 3 of their last 16 matches, and so finished runners-up in both league and cup. It still hurts to think about it!

It was only fitting that at the season's end, Jimmy Adamson was voted "Footballer of the Year". When he finally stood down from playing in April 1964, he was by far the most senior man on the club's books, having played in a total of 486 first team games. Another record which he holds is that of playing in 52 FA Cup Ties – more than any other Burnley player. And at the risk of repetition, let it be stated again that he was the last Burnley player to captain a First Division Championship team, as well as the last Claret to lead an FA Cup Final team out at Wembley.

He went on to become a coach and manager, even declining the England post. But whenever anyone writes about the history of Burnley F.C., the name of Jimmy Adamson will always be to the fore – a true Claret.

Joe ANDERSON

1920-23

Centre Forward
121 league games
64 goals

JOE ANDERSON

Joe Anderson came to Burnley to do a job. It was a big job – maybe the biggest in football. He had to follow Bert Freeman. Freeman the English international, Freeman the record goal scorer, Freeman, the man whose goal had won the FA Cup in 1914.

"Joe Andy" as he soon became known at Turf Moor arrived at the club from Scottish club Clydebank in March 1920. He was not a big man, but solidly built. Freeman was certainly the classier footballer, and when "Andy" arrived at Burnley, the great Bert Freeman simply moved over to the inside right position. Indeed Freeman never regained his centre-forward spot, such was the effect of "Joe Andy" in his new team. The team that saw Joe Andy make his first team debut read: Dawson; Smelt, Halley; Bassnett, Boyle and Watson;

Nesbitt, Freeman, Anderson, Lindsay and Mosscrop. Within a fortnight, Joe had scored his first goal for the team; within a month, he had his first hat-trick. He finished that first season with six goals in his first eight games! That season, the club were league runners-up. But the best was yet to come!

When people talk of the "old school" of centre forwards, it is usually players of the "Joe Andy" school that they are picturing. Shoulder charging, especially of the goalkeeper, was allowed and even encouraged in the twenties, and many a goalkeeper found himself and the ball in the back of the net following an Anderson charge.

1920-21 began disappointingly with three defeats. But then Joe and the team hit form. He scored winning goals against Middlesbrough, Bradford and Tottenham, and equalisers against Chelsea and Oldham. By mid December, the Clarets were top of Division One. Christmas 1920 was a particularly happy one for Joe as he scored two in a minute against Preston, and then on Christmas Day, he scored four in the 6-0 home win over Sheffield United. When the New Year of 1921 was heralded in, "Joe Andy" had 23 goals to his credit, more than any Burnley player had scored in all the previous season.

Burnley went to Leicester in the FA Cup and Joe scored four in the 7-3 victory – 19 goals in 25 games! He got another seven goals in the next two games – two against Q.P.R. in the FA Cup Tie, and five when Burnley beat Villa 7-1 at home. It is a fact that from December to February, "Joe Andy" scored 19 goals in the space of 9 games! Surely a club record? In the Villa game, even against the famed England goalkeeper Sam Hardy, Joe was unstoppable. The *Burnley News* recorded that as the referee prepared to blow his whistle for full-time, "Hardy with a look of disgust and weariness came out of his goal – never bothered to stop Anderson getting his fifth, and walked straight off the pitch, leaving the ball in the net!"

"One of these days, we shall lose 'Andy' in the netting!", ran a Burnley cartoon the following week. It was about this time that there was a newcomer in the Burnley side. "Joe Andy" was given a monkey wearing the Burnley colours as a mascot, and for several games, it would make its appearance before the game, and climb upon the crossbar.

There were set backs of course. On 12 February, Burnley met

Derby County at Turf Moor. They had a noted goalkeeper called Lawrence who it seemed took an immediate dislike to Joe (and his monkey!). Anderson and Lawrence had a battle royal that day, and my father often recalled the game. But let the Burnley paper of the day recall the events: "Anderson, in one of Burnley's rather infrequent raids, after 10 minutes play, attempted to tackle Lawrence the goalkeeper, who had the ball. The goalkeeper swinging round, caught Anderson in the face with his elbow, and in the stomach with his knee, and laid him out. He had to be carried off and attended to, and for a long time after his return, he staggered about like one completely dazed. A second time he was bowled over with a knock on the head, and then finally, about 10 minutes from the final, he was struck with the ball in the stomach and had to be carried off for the rest of the game."

My uncle described "Joe Andy" in the following terms: "He was a mediocre ball player, little better than a semi-pro. He had a few schoolboy tricks, hardly any right foot, but a good solid left foot. With all that, he had one thing going for him at that time, he was a strong man with heavy shoulders, a man built like a buffalo, who charged like one! That was his forte, charging like a buffalo at defenceless goalkeepers. A lob would drift in towards the goalmouth, the goalie would have his eye on the ball, and Joe would come charging in with his head down and charge both goalie and ball into the net. He scored dozens of goals like that, and as many more by terrorising goalkeepers so that their eyes were as much on him as they were on the ball. It was crude and brutal, and it wasn't football. But it was effective and it won games. But Lawrence sorted him out that day!" Incidentally, Burnley beat Derby County 2-1 that day, and Joe scored the winner!

By the end of the season, Burnley were League Champions, and Joe finished with 31 goals to his credit. Really after that, the only direction had to be down! In the next two seasons, Joe scored another 35 goals for the club, but by this time "Halley, Boyle 'n' Watson" had broken up and the team just wasn't the same. In 1923, Joe left Turf Moor and returned to Clydebank.

But "Joe Andy" had done the job he came to do!

John ANGUS

1955-72

Right back
438 league games
4 goals

JOHN ANGUS

I know that I'm an old traditionalist, but in my eyes, full backs nearly always come in pairs. Arsenal had Male and Hapgood, United had Carey and Aston, and we at Burnley have had McCluggage and Waterfield, Woodruff and Mather, and, of course, Angus and Elder.

John Angus was yet another who got off the train at Burnley, having got on in the North East. He was just 17 when he first came and a year later he made his League debut for the Clarets in the home game against Everton. The team in 1956 that included the 18 year old Angus read: McDonald; Angus, Smith; Seith, Adamson, Shannon; Newlands, McIlroy, McKay, Cheesebrough, Pilkington.

For the next three seasons, John competed with David Smith for the right back spot, but by August 1959, he had made the position his own. From the very beginning, John Angus was different from the average full back. Full backs by definition in the fifties were big, strong, often hefty players, who were designed to put fear into diminutive speedy wingers. And so we had full backs of the ilk of Eddie Shimwell (Blackpool), Willie Cunningham (Preston) and Tommy Banks (Bolton). And we're not forgetting Harold Mather at Turf Moor! There were others, outside of Lancashire too!

But John Angus, though strong and a hard man to play against was cool, a competitor to respect, and a polished player. How often have the likes of myself and my mates shouted "Get rid!" when he has put his foot on the ball in his own goal area, looked around, dribbled it seems along the goal line, to distribute the ball in an entirely opposite direction from the obvious one! He only missed one game during the championship season, ironically the 6-1 drubbing by Wolves at Molineux just a month before the end of the season! (How much the team missed him that night!)

He played in 56 of the 60 first team games in 1960-61 and another 46 in the momentous 1961-62 season. All this time of course, since the Championship year, John Angus had been partnered by Alex Elder and together they proved an admirable pair. One might say"never bettered". They were in so many ways, the first pair of full backs to become"wing backs"in modern terms. John was an ever present in the often overlooked 62-63 season, when the club finished third, and as the old 59-60 team gradually broke up, he was the last remaining"survivor". (Elder and Miller stayed on until 1967, but John carried on for another five seasons after that!)

A curious thing occurred in October 1964, during the game against Arsenal at Highbury. Being a defender, John's goal-scoring rate was zero, until that game. Being injured, he was put in the forwards, and he scored twice! (A word of explanation to our younger readers! Before substitutes were allowed, injured players were often put"up front", usually on the wing. The alternative was to play on with 10 men – hence the old phrase"Come on the 10 men!")

By this time, John Angus had received many honours. After his two England Youth caps, he made numerous appearances for the England Under 23's team and the Football League, before gaining an England cap in the 1961 match against Austria. Our last sight of the great man in a Burnley jersey was on the occasion in 1973 of the John Angus Testimonial Match at Turf Moor. That night, the veterans like Jimmy McIlroy, Tommy Cummings, Brian Miller and, of course, John Angus played the Youth team, with prospects like Brian Flynn and Terry Pashley. And the Second Division Champions of 72-73 played a team of recently transferred Clarets like Coates, Kindon, and Thomas. But the night certainly belonged to John Angus.

There are not many players who have played in three decades – Jerry Dawson comes immediately to mind, Tommy Cummings too, but John Angus was there, in the 50's, the 60's and the 70's. Altogether he totalled 520 first team games, which puts him third in the all-time list of Burnley players with the most appearances.

John Angus remains an icon to anyone who would aspire to be vintage Claret!

George BEEL

1923-32

Centre forward
316 league games
178 goals

GEORGE BEEL

If it's goals you're after, then this is your man. Never before and never since has anyone scored goals quite so much for Burnley as this man – George Beel.

George was, in the words of his friend and fellow Claret, Fred Blinkhorn, "an honest to goodness footballer". During his time at Turf Moor, he occupied all three inside forward positions, and merely the fact that he has held the individual league scoring record of 35 goals in a season for well over 75 years gives him a claim to a place in any selection of "all time great" Clarets.

During his time with Burnley, George scored 178 League goals, and that is also the club aggregate record for any player. Despite his great scoring feats (he also recorded more hat-tricks in his career than any other Burnley player), George never achieved any major honours. An England reserve was his only representative calling, and most of his seasons at Turf Moor were spent fighting relegation.

George came to Turf Moor in 1923, when the club was in serious decline. The days when Burnley finished second, first and third in Division One were over, and the club were now in the bottom half of the League. George arrived from Chesterfield, and played in the last game of the season, at home against Birmingham. That debut on 5 May 1923 was not a happy one. Burnley were beaten 2-0 and so finished in 15th place in the final table (their lowest position in Division One since 1900.) The team that day read: Moorwood; Smelt, Evans; Watson, Bassnett, Emerson; Greenhalgh, Kelly, Beel, Cross and Weaver.

George didn't take long to score his first goal, in the first game of the following season, and he had a fairly good first 12 months, scoring 21 goals. The club finished 17th that season. Goodness knows what might have happened but for George's supply of goals! After "Joe Andy" left in October, George became the regular No. 9. The following season was an ordinary one by his standards, scoring only 10 times. Indeed, he wasn't even top scorer, one of the few seasons that happened during his stint at Burnley. (And the club sank to 19th in the League!)

In 1926-26, Bob Kelly left the club. George Beel had been superbly served by both Kelly on the right and Benny Cross on the left. However, George seemed to benefit even more by Kelly's successor, Jackie Bruton, on the right wing. He also was richly blessed by the talents of Louis Page on the left wing. Both Bruton and Page later became English international wingers. Yet, despite this great abundance of talent (Burnley had seven international players in their team that season – Dawson, McCluggage, Waterfield, Hill, Kelly, Page and Bruton, the club just escaped relegation, finishing 20th in the League.

1926-27 saw George beginning to find his true form, when he scored another 27 goals. These included hat-tricks against Newcastle, Bolton and Tottenham, whilst he scored twice against both Everton and Liverpool. In the first five games that season, George scored nine times!

But it was in 1927-28 that the records started to tumble. He scored two hat-tricks against Derby and Sheffield United, whilst he netted a couple on another seven occasions. He finished with 35 league goals, by far a club record. He was almost as proficient the next year, when he scored 32. That year, 1928-29, George scored four hat-tricks – against Newcastle, (away) Birmingham (away), Portsmouth and Leeds. He also got two against Newcastle, Villa, Liverpool and Cardiff. Nevertheless, despite George's 65 goals in 80 league games, the Clarets still managed to finish in 19th position in the League for two seasons running.!

For the best part of half a dozen seasons, Burnley had finished just a few points away from relegation. For two seasons, they escaped by a single point. And their escape was almost entirely due to George Beel's scoring record – by 1929, he had scored over 140 goals within six seasons.

It simply couldn't continue. It only needed George to lose form or be injured, and the club would sink. And that is what happened in 1929-30. George had a very modest season, only scoring 10 times, and the club were relegated.

In Division Two, George Beel again scored as regular as clockwork – in a period of 12 games, he scored 13 goals. And then he was gone, back to his native Lincoln City. In the 75 years that have passed since then, no Burnley footballer has remotely come anywhere near to any of George Beel's records, nor perhaps his ratio of scoring more than once every two games (for 10 seasons!). How we could do with him today!

Adam BLACKLAW

1954-67

Goalkeeper
318 league games

ADAM BLACKLAW

Older Clarets fans can still be heard discussing Adam Blacklaw! What would have happened to him, but for the injury to Colin McDonald? Would he ever have made the first team? And, was he a better goalkeeper than McDonald himself?

Certainly the injury to Colin McDonald in March 1959 changed more lives than just that of the unlucky McDonald. And one of those changed lives was that of Adam Blacklaw. Until then, Adam's first team appearances had been limited to the times when first-teamer McDonald was either injured or on international duty. He had signed for Burnley as a 17 year old in 1954, and made his debut for the first team when he was only 18. The team that memorable day in December 1956 was against Cardiff City at Turf Moor, and the day was memorable because of the fog and the murky conditions;

Blacklaw; Angus, Winton; Seith, Adamson, Miller; Newlands, McIlroy, Shannon, Cheesebrough, Pilkington. Burnley won the game 6-2 in front of the season's lowest gate of 10,118 – the lowest since the war, and the lowest for the next eight seasons. (No reflection on you Adam!) I remember being there myself, despite the firm instructions of my mother!

From Adam's rapid introduction into the first team in 1959, after McDonald's injury, he only missed three games in the next five seasons – all three were memorable occasions! The first game minus Blacklaw was the week after Easter in 1960. Burnley were quite near the top and none of us were mentioning the word "Champions" Burnley went to Blackpool and drew 1-1 with a very jittery Jim Furnell taking the injured Blacklaw's place. Our hearts were in our mouths every time Jim touched the ball (and I don't think he was so happy either!) Jim Furnell later went on to play for Liverpool and Arsenal and make over 400 league appearances, but he will never forget his debut at Bloomfield Road! (And that was the day that Spurs went to Wolves and won and so opened up the way to the title for Burnley).

The second "minus Blacklaw" game was the League Cup Tie at Brentford in 1960 It was the first year of the new League Cup and Burnley weren't too happy in playing for it. They already had the League, the FA Cup and the European Cup to contend with!. (Altogether, the first team played 60 games that season!) So they went to Brentford and amazed everyone in the country by playing a full reserve team – Furnell; Smith, Marshall; Walker, Talbut, Scott; Meredith, White, Lochhead, Fenton and Harris. As the eleven team changes were read out over the Brentford loudspeaker, a chorus of booing greeted each name – a totally unknown happening in those days. Anyway, after all the jeers, Burnley came away with a 1-1 draw. (and eventually reached the Semi Final!)

And the third "minus Blacklaw" game was the famous League game against Chelsea, the same season, when once again, because of having to play so many matches, the club fielded an entire reserve team. In a quite amazing game, the second string drew 4-4 and only a late Jimmy Greaves goal saved the day for Chelsea! We seem to have digressed a little from Adam Blacklaw's story, but the above examples only serve to illustrate how regular he was for those years "between the sticks".

To succeed, a player like McDonald must have been an unenviable task, yet this was Adam Blacklaw's lot. Hefty, uncompromising, daring and spectacular, Blacklaw was quite different from McDonald, and yet over the years, many people came to prefer him to the unfortunate McDonald.

For me, and many other Burnley fans, two games stand out in our memories of Adam Blacklaw; both cup ties, both drawn. In 1960-61, Burnley drew 0-0 at Hillsbrough against Sheffield Wednesday in the Sixth Round, and that day it was Sheffield Wednesday v Adam Blacklaw! How Burnley managed to get through that game, no-one but Blacklaw will ever know! The following season, and Burnley were facing Fulham in the Semi Final at Villa Park. Burnley were very much favourites at the top of the league, whilst Fulham were fighting against relegation. But it was Fulham who all but won the game that day, and only Adam Blacklaw stood between the unfortunate Fulham and Wembley.

So many games, so many memories come flooding back when anyone recalls the days of Adam Blacklaw – Adam at Rheims, Adam at Wembley, Adam in Naples. But one event outrides all the others. February 1963 and the FA Cup Replay at Anfield against Liverpool. The score was 1-1 very late in extra time, and we Clarets fans were very confident of beating Liverpool anywhere they wanted to play us in the next replay. "And then, with the referee looking at his watch and the ball in Blacklaw's hands, Adam Blacklaw could have chosen to do any number of things when he received a back pass from Alex Elder in the dying seconds of extra time. He decided to boot the ball up field from the edge of his penalty area – and succeeded only in scoring a direct hit on Liverpool leader, Ian St. John, lurking tenaciously little more than a couple of arm's length away. The ball rebounded past Blacklaw, St. John flashed after it, and would undoubtedly have put it into the net had not Blacklaw in complete and utter desperation, rugby tackled him from behind. A penalty of course, and left back Moran put his side into Round Five with a safe, sure spot kick in a fantastic, sensational last minute climax.

That was the nightmare, freakish ending to Burnley's cup hopes for another season – a finish that will live for ever in the memory of 58,000 stunned spectators. A tragic, terrible, careless mistake though by Blacklaw, who understandably enough, looked close to tears at the final whistle, only TWENTY SECONDS later." *(Burnley Express)* I was stood right behind Adam that night, on the Kop amid 10,000 Liverpool fans. How I felt for him!

Few players bring back such vivid memories as Adam Blacklaw. Altogether the Scot played in 383 first team games, making 194 consecutive appearances at one time. He played for the Scotland Under 23's team and three times for the full International team. Clarets don't come any better or braver than Adam Blacklaw.

Tommy BOYLE

1911-23

Centre half
210 league games
36 goals

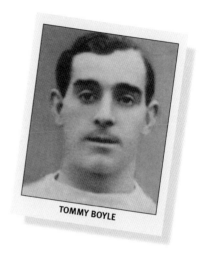

TOMMY BOYLE

Tommy Boyle was already a national figure when he arrived at Turf Moor in October 1911. He was captain of the Barnsley team, and part of the Glendinning, Boyle and Utley half back line that had faced Newcastle United in the 1910 FA Cup Final. He signed for the club on 1 October 1911, for the highest fee that the club had ever paid for a player – £1,150. By coincidence, his first game for his new club was against his old club, Barnsley on 4 October 1911. The team read; Dawson; Reid, Bamford; Swift, Boyle, Watson; Morley, Hodgson, Freeman, Mountford, Mayson. It could be said, that the transfer of Tommy Boyle was the most important signing that Burnley ever made from another club.

After having made his name for Barnsley, it was surely nothing compared to the fame that was going to be attached to his name over the next decade. Captaining Burnley in their first ever Cup Final, receiving the Cup from the King himself, playing for England, and leading hs team to their first ever League Championship title, were only some of the highlights in the life of Tommy Boyle. He was never a talkative man, and his motto could be said to be "Deeds not words!" People like my grandad remembered him for his superb heading ability, and also for his wide swinging passes out to the wings. He should be remembered too for his guts and courage, as in the game against Arsenal in January 1922: "In a collision, Boyle received a very bad cut on the forehead, but with commendable pluck, he refused to leave the field, and continued playing with the linesman's handkerchief serving as a bandage. On one occasion, he had hard luck not scoring, as it was due to the blood trickling over his eyes that he misdirected a strong shot. At the close, he had to have several stitches inserted." (Burnley Express)

But my grandad remembered him best simply for his captaincy and leadership.If he was a hard man to play against, he was equally a hard man to play for. He always demanded and got the best out of his team. Both my dad and grandad often recalled the manner in which Tommy would bellow orders across the pitch, and if the team were down, he would roll up his sleeves and clap his hands together in encouragement. His voice could be heard all over the pitch. I recall hearing from Dad how Billy Nesbitt, who was partially deaf, told of how Boyle "put the fear of God into him" by his bawdy and somewhat offensive shouting. But it worked!

From Boyle's arrival, the crowds rolled up at Turf Moor in unprecedented numbers. Three times in the 1911-12 season, the gate receipts record was shattered by hundreds of pounds. On 16 March 1912, Derby County came to Burnley. At the time, Derby complete with Steve Bloomer were lying third in Division Two, whilst Burnley were on top of the Division. The attendance was 31,000 "among whom were an unprecedented number of ladies". The receipts were another Turf Moor League record of £831. (Incidentally, by the end of the season, thanks to Burnley only winning once in their last five games, the positions were reversed and Derby finished Champions with Burnley third in the League)

The following season, Captain Boyle led his Burnley team to promotion back to the First Division, as well as to the Semi Final of the FA Cup. On their way to the Semi Final, Burnley beat Blackburn Rovers "on their own midden" 1-0, and Tommy Boyle scored the solitary goal by heading home a corner kick. Soon after that game, Burnley signed George Halley, a right half for "a large sum of money" from Bradford Park Avenue. What was significant about this move

Burnley, 1920-21 Champions

The Burnley team that broke all the records. At the front of the picture the three players at the heart of the side – the legendary "Halley, Boyle 'n' Watson".

was that it brought together for the first time, George Halley, Tommy Boyle, and Billy Watson, who have gone down in history as the legendary "Halley, Boyle 'n' Watson". They made their first appearance together against Bury when the team read: Sewell; Bamford, Jones; Halley, Boyle, Watson; Mosscrop, Lindley, Freeman, Hodgson, Mountford, The same month as George Halley arrived, Tommy Boyle made his International debut for England v Ireland.

Excitement was high in Burnley at the start of 1913-14, with the club back in Division One. Gate records were broken wherever Burnley played, and during January and February, they went eleven games without defeat. But at the same time, the club were making great progress in the FA Cup, beating South Shields, Derby County, and Bolton before meeting Sunderland in the Quarter Finals. Altogether, 49,734 people filled Turf Moor that day to see the famous Sunderland team with their stars, Ness, Cuggy, Buchan, Mordue & Co. "In the history of Burnley Football Club, it will be recorded that one of the most brilliant achievements was the victory over Sunderland." So wrote one local paper in retrospect. Burnley won 2-1, and the *"Daily News"* said: "It was a great triumph for Burnley, looked at from whatever point of view one likes. They were a great side, fore and aft. Admirably captained by that great centre-half back, Tommy Boyle, they had not a weak spot."

The Semi Final went to a replay against Sheffield United, at Everton on 1 April 1914. "The score was 0-0, when with 17 minutes to go, Nesbitt, who had scarcely played up to his true form, centred brilliantly, right to the feet of Mosscrop. Mosscrop trapped the ball and touched it back to Boyle, who espying an opening amid the players, shot the ball into the net with terrific force." It was the winning goal and Burnley were through to their first ever FA Cup Final. Said the *"Burnley News"*: "Individually, Boyle was a wonder!"

Came the Final at Crystal Palace, and Freeman's goal came 13 minutes after the interval. Tommy Boyle's voice could be heard all over the ground as he urged his team on. Twelve minutes from the end, he collapsed with a chest injury, but after treatment, he was able to continue. And so it was that two days later, Tommy Boyle, sitting in his shirt sleeves at the front of the wagonette riding through vast cheering crowds, brought the FA Cup back to Burnley.

After the War, which surely robbed the Burnley team of untold successes, the local paper reported: "Boyle is playing better than ever". He was injured for a spell, but on his return "Halley, Boyle 'n' Watson" were reunited and played together for the first time since 1914. (Incidentally, it was about this time in 1919, that the club began to be called "The Clarets" in place of their older nickname "The Turfites")

It is sometimes difficult to understand how violent the game was in those far off days, but we find a hint of it in the *"Burnley News"* in March 1920. "Personally, I do not think that Boyle looks quite fit, but for all that I regretted the action he took with regard to Peart on one occasion. One Burnley player has just finished suspension for retaliation, and the fact that Boyle had been kicked did not justify him seizing Peart by the throat!"

The 1920-21 season has gone down in history – 30 consecutive league games without defeat, etc. Tommy Boyle led the team throughout the season, as the club won the League Championship. During the season, Tommy scored seven goals himself (they were nearly all either penalties or headers!). Indeed, during his time at Turf Moor, Tommy Boyle scored 43 goals, an average of approximately, once every five games! An amazing record for a defender.

The great man eventually played his final game for Burnley in February 1922, when Arsenal were the visitors to Turf Moor. He had played 236 games for the club, despite many football injuries and some severe injuries received in the War, and had always been the born leader. Indeed, in some ways, Tommy Boyle gave his life for Burnley. His health declined to the point where he died in a local mental hospital in 1940, his illness almost certainly brought on by the consistent heading of heavy footballs.

When he retired, the local paper honoured him with the headline: "THE DEPARTURE OF BOYLE – THE GREATEST CAPTAIN THE CLUB EVER POSSESSED!"

That says it all!

Allan BROWN

1946-48

Centre half
88 league games

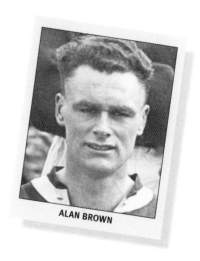

ALAN BROWN

If any individuals were responsible for Burnley's rise as a football club after the Second War, the two who come to mind are manager Cliff Britton and captain Allan Brown. It was Cliff Britton who brought Allan Brown to Burnley and it was the manager who made him captain.

Allan Brown came to Burnley just prior to the start of the 1946-47 season, and he was there in the team that won promotion from day one. He was a hard man, a strong tackler, and an inspirational captain – probably the best the club had had since the days of Tommy Boyle. Allan Brown was the king pin of what became nationally known as "the iron curtain defence". To this day, the names still roll off your tongue – Strong, Woodruff, Mather, Attwell, Brown and Bray.

The first game that Allan Brown played for Burnley was in August 1946, when the club played Coventry City at Turf Moor; 17,000 saw the following Burnley team: Strong; Woodruff, Mather; Spencer, Brown, Bray; Chew, Morris, Billingham, Potts and Kippax. It was the first time that Burnley had played in claret and blue for over ten years, as before the war, the club had turned out in white shirts and black shorts. They also wore numbers for the first time!

Burnley's football was not always pretty to watch, like say, the 59-60 team. The post war team were defensive and dour, with a "they shall not pass" approach. With Allan Brown stamping his leadership on the team, the club had some remarkable statistics. They went 16 league games without defeat between September and December, and a further 20 games without defeat starting in December. Add them together and you get 37 consecutive games with only one defeat. Even Halley, Boyle 'n' Watson didn't do that! They only conceded 29 league goals during the season, a League record. And through the entire season, Allan Brown was an ever present.

Writer and Burnley fan at the time, Jack Rosenthal described the team; "Out they came. First, striding purposefully, already in an angry mood, Allan Brown, the captain; brow furrowed, jaw set, Prometheus looking for trouble." On another occasion, Jack wrote: "Everyone was left standing by Policeman Brown, guarding his penalty area like a mother pterodactyl, and clearing every centre at least 40 yards up field with one vicious clout of his head." If we had to single out any particular games that Allan Brown played during that season, they might well be the two Semi Finals against Liverpool in the FA Cup. At that time, Liverpool were leading Division One (and they finished the season as champions!) And they had as their centre forward, the newly signed Albert Stubbins who had cost the club a record £13,000 from Newcastle. The game, played at Ewood, resulted in a 0-0 draw, but the highlight of the game was the battle between Brown and Stubbins. The biggest crowd to see Burnley that season, some 72,000 packed Maine Road to see the replay. But Brown & Co. held on to see the Clarets win through to the FA Cup Final, 1-0

And so, Allan Brown became the first Burnley captain since Tommy Boyle to lead out his team in the Cup Final; Strong; Woodruff, Mather; Attwell, Brown, Bray; Chew, Morris, Harrison, Potts and Kippax. Defeated on the day, but heroes all!

The following season, Burnley more than matched all opposition in the First Division, finishing third, and again led by Brown. In one of his last games for Burnley at Blackpool, Alan Brown tackled Mortenson, the Blackpool centre forward early on. The Blackpool trainer was needed, but Allan Brown had made his presence felt! It certainly affected the match, which Burnley went on to win 1-0. The last time I was at Bloomfield Road half a dozen years ago, a Blackpool fan asked me: "Were you here when Brown tackled Mortenson?" I ask you – nearly 60 years later and people still recall one particular tackle he made! But that was Alan Brown – hard and uncompromising, he was the pivot of a superb defence and the complete captain. What more could any Clarets fan wish for?

Jack BRUTON

1925-29

Right wing
167 league games
42 goals

JACK BRUTON

A Lancashire lad through and through John Bruton, known to the fans as "Jackie" arrived at Turf Moor in 1925. He was just 21 and very soon he made his first team debut at Turf Moor against Newcastle. The Burnley team that day read: Dawson; Fergus, Evans; Hughes, Armitage, Tresadern; Bruton, Cross, Williams, Beel, Tonner. The Burnley team was going through a time of transition after the great days four years earlier, and several of those players only played for a season or less. Despite losing that day, Jackie Bruton scored on his debut.

It was several games into the next season, 1925-26, and Burnley were struggling at the foot of Division One, before Jackie Bruton was properly reintroduced into the first team. His arrival didn't have a profound effect on the team's fortunes, because after 17 games, the club were well and truly bottom. And then they sold Bob Kelly!

Maybe the departure of Kelly forced Burnley to rely even more on their two new wingers, Jackie Bruton and Louis Page. (Sadly, it wasn't the attack that needed improvements, but rather the defence. In 1925-26, they conceded three sixes, two eights and a 10!) Both Bruton and Page were fast and tricky, skilful goal-providers for the likes of George Beel. And both could score goals freely themselves.

Season by season, Jackie Bruton became the idol of the Turf Moor terraces, with his ball control and speed; in the mid-twenties the right wing of Bruton and Cross was a revelation. 1926-27 was the best season for Burnley since 1922, when for the only time in eight seasons, the club finished higher than 15th! And maybe symbolic of that fact was that Jackie Bruton was the team's only ever present player. Indeed, he only missed something like three games in nearly four seasons.

Week after week, Bruton's brilliance shone through and Burnley scored goals like never before, averaging well over 80 goals a season for five years. By now, Jackie Bruton had assumed the mantle of the late, great Bob Kelly and the crowd worshipped him. He was chosen to represent the Football League and then in three full English internationals. Both for Burnley and now England, the sweeping runs of Jackie Bruton were becoming known throughout the land.

"The brilliance of Bruton" and "Bruton saves Burnley again" were typical headlines of those days. And then came the killer blow. It happened soon after the West Ham match in 1929 when the gate was 6,670, the lowest at a Saturday match at Turf Moor for six years. Club Secretary, Mr. A. Pickles put the situation fair and square to the public of Burnley, when he said that "unless gates improve, the club will be forced to sell players like Page, Devine and Bruton." And his words were soon followed by action, when English international and crowd favourite Jackie Bruton was transferred for about £6,000. To Blackburn Rovers!

There was a public outcry in the town. It was a repeat of the scenes when the club had sold Bob Kelly, and it foreshadowed the sale in later years of Jimmy McIlroy. As an immediate result of Bruton's sale, the club won only three games in their last 15 fixtures and were relegated. Fred Blinkhorn, friend and playing colleague of Jackie Bruton's said to me in later years: "It took 20 years and a World War for Burnley to get over the selling of Jackie Bruton!" He wasn't the first Claret to go. And he certainly wasn't the last. But Jackie Bruton, the flying winger, was most certainly, one of the best that we ever lost!

Ralph COATES

1963-71

Midfield and Forward
214 league games
26 goals

RALPH COATES

What Jimmy McIlroy was to many people in the late fifties, so Ralph Coates assumed the magician's mantle in the next decade. Some people even preferred Coates to McIlroy because of his speed, his ball control, and his almost aggressive attitude towards the game. (Not that he was rough, for like "Mac", Ralph Coates was one of the game's gentlemen). But Ralph had an enthusiasm to get involved with the game that made him one of Burnley's leading personalities of the sixties.

Ralph Coates got off the North East train in 1961 and became a professional with the club in 1963. He made his first team debut when he was only 18 in the week before Christmas 1964. The game was at home against Sheffield United and the Burnley team read: Blacklaw; Smith, Elder; Todd, Miller, O'Neil; Towers, Coates, Irvine, Bellamy and Price. That day, Ralph stood in for the injured Andy Lochhead and that was his role in that first season – stand in. He played just seven games, but played in three positions!

By the start of the following season, Ralph had made the left wing spot his own, and there he stayed for the next three seasons. What a revelation he was! How many times, the crowd have gasped at his speed off the mark? How many times did a piece of brilliance from Ralph Coates swing round a game that had seemed lost? By 1967, he had become a regular England Under 23's player, and over the next few years, he represented the Football League on several occasions.

Though he had become the club's number one number eleven, we saw him at his greatest in a deeper midfield role. In 1968-69, he played in four varying positions – right half, right wing, inside right and left, before settling in at No. 8, the old McIlroy role for his last two seasons with the club. For me, Ralph Coates followed in the Jimmy McIlroy and Ray Pointer tradition – it was worth the entrance fee just to watch him alone!

Though a stocky figure, he could be amazingly fast and his skill made him stand out in any team. He regularly grabbed the headlines, such as in the 5-2 drubbing of Leicester City in 1966-67: "COATES – THE EXECUTIONER IN GREAT TEAM DISPLAY" By 1969, Ralph was by far the club's outstanding player, despite his team's disappointing performances. Maybe the club's form was due to inexperience, because towards Christmas that season, Burnley fielded their youngest ever team in the First Division: Mellor (22), Nulty (20), Latcham (26), Docherty (19), Merrington (24), O'Neil (25), Coates (23), Thomas (19), Murray (21), Dobson (21) and Kindon (18). Clarets fans of that generation are still puzzled as to how a team fielding the likes of Angus, Thomas, Coates and Dobson, not to mention Waldron, Kindon and Docherty (with Leighton James as a reserve!) could even contemplate relegation. Actually no-one ever contemplated it, so maybe it was the club's complacency which helped to send us down?

By then, Ralph had become an England player, and there was a great outcry in the town when he was omitted from the final England squad for the 1970 Mexico World Cup. It was inevitable on the club's relegation in 1971, that some big city club would move in to sign Coates and the inevitable happened when the week after relegation, Ralph Coates was signed by Tottenham for £190,000.(How often have we Burnley fans seen our heroes go? My grandad had seen Crabtree and Hillman leave; my dad remembered Kelly, Hill and Bruton departing; I have seen McIlroy, Connelly, Morgan and Coates go, whilst my son had enjoyed watching the likes of Glenn Little and Robbie Blake before their departure. There have been many others, but it still hurts!) But Ralph Coates remains at Turf Moor in our minds and memories. We've seen some great players at Burnley, and Ralph was indeed one of the best! And yes, it is quite true that Ralph

Coates after receiving some heavy treatment from the Rovers defenders in 1966, sat down on the ball, half inviting any Rovers player to come and take it off him! That was Ralphie Coates for you!

John CONNELLY

1956-64

Right wing
215 league games
86 goals

JOHN CONNELLY

Billy Gray and Doug Newlands were both fine right wingers in the 1950's. They were a hard act to follow. But John Connelly not only followed them with distinction. He outshone them both.

He first came to Turf Moor in 1956 and made his debut as a 19 year old in March 1957. The game was away at Leeds, and that day, the Burnley team read: McDonald, Angus, Winton; Seith, Miller, Shannon; Newlands, McIlroy, Shackleton, Cheesebrough and Connelly. From the start, Connelly could be seen as different. Not a dribbler, but very fast and direct. And he packed a shot too.

It was another two seasons before he was able to establish himself in the first team as a regular, due to the skills of Doug Newlands. But by October 1958, John had well and truly arrived, and the right wing position was his for the next five seasons. He was a favourite with the crowd from the beginning, and the Turf Moor thousands often rose to his sweeping runs, when with great speed he would cut in from the wing, to test the goalkeeper with a powerful shot. He formed an admirable partner to Jimmy McIlroy, and the two complemented each other in fine style.

He scored goals freely and in only his first season he was the second highest goalscorer. The following season,1959-60,the

Championship season, one of the many highlights to savour was the wing play of John Connelly. He set out his stall early in the season, scoring four in the first three games. He went on to score two against Everton, two against Newcastle (away), two against West Ham (away) and a hat-trick against Arsenal (away). That was what it was like, kids!

By now, he was already an England regular, and scoring for his country too. Unfortunately, before the season ended, John was injured and missed seven games in the run in. Thank goodness his stand in was no duffer himself, for young Trevor Meredith not only scored three times in his seven games, but eventually scored the winner at Maine Road to bring the League title back to Burnley at the season's end.

Despite missing eight games, John Connelly still scored twenty five goals and ended up top scorer. It was the highest total by any Burnley winger since the 26 scored by Louis Page in 1925-26.

He scored another twenty the next season, but such was the Clarets scoring rate that he was only the third highest at the end of the season. The goals came thick and fast – two each against Arsenal, Blackburn (away), Man Utd, Bolton (away), and Spurs (away). But mainly from TV and video, he is also remembered for his very typical goal against Rheims in the European Cup.

And another 20 in 1961-62. They came in regular fashion – two against Leicester (away), a hat-trick against Fulham (away), two against Wolves, two more against Sheffield Wednesday. I confess here and now before you all, that like most Clarets fans that season, I took these results and goals for granted! September 1962 was one of the greatest months in the history of the club. Seven games, seven wins (four away from home!). The Clarets scored 27 goals in one month, including away wins at Manchester City (3-1), Birmingham (6-2), Leicester (6-2), and Fulham (5-3). John Connelly played in them all and scored six in a month! Those were the days, my friends!

For me, the best Connelly performance was the following season, 1962-63 when the Clarets went to Old Trafford and beat Manchester United 5-2, with John getting a hat-trick! I was there that day, and pride doesn't adequately describe my feelings of being a Claret fan! Though others who were fortunate to be at White Hart Lane may suggest the Clarets 4-4 draw with Spurs in 1960 was the best of all Clarets days, when John Connelly scored two and hit a post! Phew!

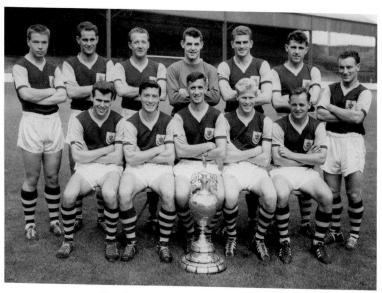

Burnley, 1959-60 League Champions

Left to right, back row: Alex Elder (debut that season), Jimmy Robson, Tommy Cummings, Adam Blacklaw, Brian Miller, John Angus, Trevor Meredith (scored the winning goal that won the title in the last match). Left to right, front row: John Connelley (top scorer), Jimmy McIlroy, Jimmy Adamson (captain), Ray Pointer and Brian Pilkington.

1963-64 saw the emergence of Willie Morgan from the Reserve team, and John Connelly moved over to the left wing to accommodate him. The goals continued to come – two against Blackburn (away), two more against both Everton and West Brom. And the caps continued to come his way. (John Connelly received more England caps than any other Burnley player since the war, and is second only to Bob Kelly in the all-time list).

It was sad, but certainly no surprise when Manchester United moved in with a bid of £56,000 at the end of the 63-64 season. (These days it would be millions!) During his time at Turf Moor, (265 games and over a century of goals) John Connelly was undisputedly one of the most exciting players on the pitch. He had the speed of Kindon, the enthusiasm of Coates, and the shooting power of Lochhead. Such was John Connelly – as good as they get!.

James CRABTREE

1882-95

Half back
72 league games
9 goals

JAMES CRABTREE

The first time I ever heard of James W. Crabtree was from my grandad. Crabtree, I was told, was the finest footballer of his day. He played for Burnley and he came from Burnley. That was what stuck in my mind – that Crabtree whoever he was, had come from Burnley. My grandad seemed to have seen him, I know not where or when, but grandad was certainly impressed by the man.

I myself now know a lot more about James Crabtree, and like a lot of other things I only wish that I had talked a bit more with my grandad about him. Yes indeed, James Crabtree was born in Burnley, and from the very beginnings of the club, James Crabtree was there.

On 14 October 1882, Burnley played their first competitive match, a Lancashire Cup game. The following week, the *"Burnley Express"* summarily reported: "Burnley v Astley Bridge. On Saturday afternoon last, these two clubs met on the ground of the former at Calder Vale to contest in the first round for the Lancashire Challenge Cup. Astley Bridge had it all their own way throughout, and won the game by eight goals to none. A large company assembled to witness the match. This is the first year the Burnley club has played Association rules. Team: Goal, H.Walton; full backs, S.Hargreaves and A.Birley; half backs J.Crabtree and G.Waddington; centres, W.Brown and S.Barlow; right wing, T.Midgeley (captain) and F.Slater; left wing, J.Marsland and T.French. We can only estimate that James Crabtree was still in his very early teens.

The local paper a fortnight later reported that Blackburn Rovers had beaten Burnley 10-0 at Calder Vale, and once again James

Crabtree played, this time on the right wing. Crabtree later recalled how he also played against Preston at Deepdale in a "friendly". On that occasion he played outside left, and once when he tried to pass full back Bob Howarth, Howarth gave him a shoulder charge. Crabtree said it was a fair charge, but it had the result that he was knocked 10 yards under the rails on the stand side. He said later that he thought his last hour had come! But the lad of 16 got up and finished the game. At the time, he got 2/6d a week – with charges like that thrown in for nothing! Even James Crabtree thought it was not enough, so he asked for 4/- and got it.

Five months after the Rovers game, there was a match report of the Burnley v Haslingden match: "A word of commendation is certainly due to all the players who were in grand form, more especially Smith and Crabtree, who have the making of two good young players, if they will only practice, and who on Saturday played very creditably". Quite a prophet writing there for the *"Burnley Express"*!

Soon afterwards, James Crabtree asked for a pay rise to 7/6d, but because the club refused to pay such an exorbitant salary. he went to Rossendale. He returned to Burnley and made his league debut in September 1889. The game was against Accrington at Turf Moor, and the team read: Cox; White, Bury; Keenan, Lang, McFetteridge; Duckworth, Haresnape, Campbell, Heyes, and Crabtree. His second game was at West Brom, and though Burnley were crushed 6-1, it was Crabtree, almost certainly the youngest player on the field who scored for Burnley. The following week, Burnley with Crabtree went to Preston and were again heavily beaten 6-0 by the reigning league champions.

In 1891-92, we believe that young James was playing for Heywood, but the following season he came home again and spent the season playing for Burnley. (In those days, the team played in blue and white stripes and were known locally as "the Royalites". This was because in 1886, Burnley had played a friendly against Bolton Wanderers in front of Prince Albert, in aid of the new Victoria Hospital.)

For the next three seasons, James Crabtree played in the first team at Turf Moor. Altogether he played in 77 first team games and scored nine goals. He had originally begun as a full back, but during his career he performed with great prowess in every position on the field, including goalkeeper. In 1895, the Turf Moor club got their names in the history books by being involved in the very first transfer fee. Once again, young James had got into a dispute with the club over his salary, and Burnley, objecting to pay the "exorbitant terms" he requested, sold him to Aston Villa.

By now James Crabtree was playing for England – alongside the likes of Bob Howarth (his old Preston adversary), Billy Bassett (West Brom) and Steve Bloomer (Derby Co.) and obviously he felt that we was worth more than 4/- a game! We don't know what Villa paid him, but they paid Burnley £250 for his services.

At Villa Park, James Crabtree captained the team that won the double, winning four League championships and two Cup Finals. He captained England too. Loyal to the core and afraid of no-one, James Crabtree played in all five defensive positions for England. With this sort of record, it is no wonder that over the years, he has been described on several occasions as the greatest footballer of all time.

And as my grandad told me so often – he came from Burnley!

Tommy CUMMINGS

1947-63

Centre half, full back
434 league games
3 goals

TOMMY CUMMINGS

Yet another, who came to Burnley on the North East train, Tommy Cummings was just 20 when he made his first team debut at Maine Road in December 1948. The great team of 46-47 was beginning to break up and one of the first to go was captain Allan Brown. He left for Notts County in October 1948 and the club had a problem to tackle. Who could follow him? Bob Johnston from the Reserves was tried and then even Arthur Woodruff. But then, the young

Burnley, c1954

A curious Burnley squad about 1954. Curious, because David Cargill (back row right) only ever played five games for the first team and also because Gus Alexander (front row right) never made a first team appearance in his six years at the club. Probably a close season touring side? Back row, left to right: Stevenson, McIlroy, Holden, Frank Hill (manager), Cummings, Shannon, Cargill. Front row, left to right: Adamson, Winton, McDonald, Mather and Alexander. Only Adamson, Cummings and McIlroy would still be around to celebrate Burnley's Championship title win six years later.

Cummings was given his chance, and how he took it! For the next eight years, other than when absent through injury, nobody took his place.

The Burnley team facing Manchester City on that day in December 1948 read: Strong; Loughran, Mather; Attwell, Cummings, Bray; Chew, Morris, Harrison, Potts and Hays. By the end of that season, Tommy Cummings was a well established part of the Burnley defence. He was a totally different style of player from the hard man Brown. Tommy was fast, very fast. I would suggest that he was one of the fastest players ever to play for Burnley. (What a fascinating 100 metres race that would be – players like Jackie Bruton and Louis Page up against the likes of Cummings, Connelly and Kindon! But I digress!)

One of the greatest joys I have ever had whilst watching Burnley over the years was seeing Tommy Cummings, week by week, facing up to some of the several fine centre forwards of his day – Lofthouse of Bolton, Ford of Sunderland, Mortenson of Blackpool, Taylor of Manchester United and Milburn of Newcastle. They were always events to look forward to and relish. They were all clever and fast. And so was Tommy! Indeed, in Tommy's second match, he travelled back to his native North East to face Newcastle and the redoubtable Jackie Milburn. That day, Tommy earned the local press headlines which heralded: "CUMMINGS EARNED HONOURS!.HE HELD MILBURN". The task of holding Jackie Milburn, then England's speedy centre forward and taking a point from League leaders Newcastle on their own ground, was one worthy of headlines in 1949. Within two seasons, Tommy played for the Football League team, and was selected as reserve for the England team, and later the England "B" team.

Tommy Cummings only scored three goals during his lengthy career at Turf Moor, but two of them came in 1951-52. He scored one that earned a 2-2 draw with Wolves at Turf Moor, but it was the second that has gone down in history. I was there myself, but I'll let the *"Burnley Express"* tell the story: "As the seconds were ticking out for a draw, Cummings robbed Milburn just outside the Burnley penalty area and started his great run. He beat seven players and the Newcastle defenders expected him to pass. He feinted to do so by veering right in the United territory, then came in for goal. From about 18 yards, he hit the ball just inside the post past Simpson. Instantly, all Turf Moor rose in a sustained roar." And stood with me in the old Enclosure, my dad turned to me and said: "That's the greatest goal you'll ever see in your life, son!" He was right, and I can still wipe away a tear at the memory.

Over the years, the half back line at Burnley changed from Attwell, Cummings, and Bray to Adamson, Cummings and Attwell; then to Adamson, Cummings,and Seith to Adamson, Cummings and Shannon.and then into the sixties, to Adamson, Cummings, and Miller. We saw some truly great wing halves, but always, there was Tommy in the middle. He was there when Jimmy McIlroy arrived in 1950, he played at the Elliott-Cunningham duel with North End in 1952; he was there for the great Cup Tie with Manchester United in 1954; 1956-58 were a bit of a washout for Tommy due to injury, but there he was at the end of the decade, in the crucial last match at Maine Road in the midst of an Adamson, Cummings and Miller half back line, helping to win the title.

Later in his career, Tommy Cummings converted to right back (such was Burnley's mid field strength), and he played many times from 1956 onwards in that role. He even, when the need was there, played several games in the left back position. Altogether 479 appearances in a career that rose to a climax with the League title. My grandad had worshipped Tommy Boyle. My dad grew up watching Jack Hill. But for me the best centre half since the war was always Tommy Cummings.

Steve DAVIS

1991-2003

Defender, midfielder
321 league games
42 goals

STEVE DAVIS

It would be no exaggeration to say that Steve Davis was by far the leading Burnley F.C. personality of the 1990's. And in a decade that included Chris Waddle, Ian Wright and Paul Gascoigne as well as several well established Turf Moor figures like Payton and Little, that is no small claim.

He came to Turf Moor first of all on loan from his club at Southampton. That was in November 1989 and he was named as sub against Lincoln City. He played in the first team for the first time the next week in the home game against Grimsby, when the Clarets team read: Pearce, Measham, Hardy, Farrell, Davis, Davis (S),White, Mumby, Futcher, Jakub, Bent. At the time, the club were a regular bottom half of the Fourth Division side, far removed from the glory days, and still wincing at the thought of the Orient game just two years earlier. Steve immediately made an impression on the locals, but sadly returned South after the loan. Less than two seasons later,

Steve Davis

Steve Davis – combative, calm under pressure, good anticipation, read the game well, strong in defence, scorer of great goals, reliable, consistent – had all the qualities which endeared him to the Burnley faithful.

in August 1991, manager Frank Casper paid £60,000 to bring him back North. It was a bargain! He was tall and strong, and with good anticipation, able to read the game well. His signing was to prove a major asset in Burnley's drive for promotion. Right from the start, he slotted into the team. And before very long, the Turf Moor crowd were getting used to his calmness at the back and his readiness to go on long runs down the middle.

For the next four seasons, Steve rarely missed a match and he was consistently outstanding. 1991-92 was a memorable time for both Steve and the Clarets. The new look defence of Measham, Jakub,

Pender and Davis brought a new stability to the team, and that season they only conceded 43 goals, the best figure since 1973 when the club had topped Division Two! The Pender-Davis pairing brought the best out of them both, and the team would sometimes go three games without conceding a goal. Steve could score goals too and he finished the season with eight goals to his credit, among them being the 30 yard shot that he drilled in against Wigan in the Rumbelows Cup. By the end of his first season at Turf Moor, Steve Davis had helped the club win promotion after seven years in Division Four. For himself, he was chosen by his fellow professionals as a member of the Fourth Division "All Star" team.

1992-93 was a consolidation season in Division Two, after the excitement of the previous season. It was just as well, for there was even more excitement to follow in 1993-94. By the summer of 1993, rumours abounded that Steve Davis was being hunted by such teams as Wolves, Liverpool and Nottm Forest, but fortunately, they came to nought, when he signed a new two year deal with the Clarets. Soon afterwards, Steve completed his first hundred games for the Turf Moor team. By now, his partnership with captain John Pender at the heart of the Burnley defence had become one of the most respected pairings in the Second Division. It was certainly a major factor in Burnley's continued success in the League.

Though automatic promotion was not realised, the Clarets found themselves battling through the Play-Offs against Plymouth, before beating Stockport County at Wembley in the Final. Unbelievable scenes greeted the team, both at Wembley and the following day in Burnley as Steve Davis and his team-mates received the plaudits of the Turf Moor faithful. But the run of success came to a sudden halt in 1994-95 when the Clarets finished in the bottom four of Division One, and were back in Division Two within a season.

In no way could any blame be attached to Steve Davis, as his weekly performances were as reliable and consistent as ever. Indeed were it not for his goals which earned draws against Stoke, Bolton and Grimsby and which helped win matches against Charlton, Sheffield United, Southend and Derby, the club would have been relegated long before the season's end. It must have been particularly disappointing for Steve, as he had been made club captain. Pressures were growing on the club as they fought to keep Steve at Turf Moor. In October, Leeds United reportedly bid £1m plus for his services.

This was followed by a bid by Chelsea, but manager Jimmy Mullen turned it down, saying that Steve was not for sale, not even for £2m! However, the rumours continued throughout the season with Blackburn and Sunderland being linked with his name.

The return to Division Two at the end of the 1994-95 season brought all the speculation to a head, as Burnley accepted a fee of £750,000 (a club record) for their talented captain. He had proved to be too good for Division Two and so First Division Luton Town stepped in for his signature. It was a sad day for us all when big Steve left Turf Moor, and it didn't mean that the club were improving their playing staff.

For the next few seasons, the rumour mongers had a field day, often suggesting that our much missed Steve might return to Turf Moor, but there simply wasn't the money available. But the dreams came true for the club and its fans in December 1998 when big Steve was brought back to Brunshaw Road by the new Chairman, Barry Kilby. The fee paid to Luton was £750,000, the same fee we had received. And we felt he was still a bargain!

Obviously, now in his thirties, Steve Davis wasn't quite the same player he had previously been. Some of his speed may have gone, but he was still there at the right time, making that tackle, going up to meet that corner, and breaking through opposing midfields. Within 12 months, his presence was having its old effect on the team as again they challenged for promotion out of the Second Division. By now in 1999-2000, it was business as usual as Steve, now club captain again, led his team back to the First Division. This time though in 2000-01 it was a far more consistent team that kept up with, and at one time, led the pace in Division One.

For two seasons, the club missed out on the Play Offs by first, two points, (2000-01) and the year after, by a single goal. In his last couple of seasons, Steve had a string of injuries, which regularly kept him out of the side. And naturally the team suffered along with big Steve. More than once, he was brought back into the squad before he was fit. And a succession of premature come backs for the sake of the club no doubt hastened on his final game.

Since Steve Davis left Turf Moor in 2003, the club has never finished in the top half of the division, and the struggle for survival has become more intense. But we wouldn't be where we are in The Championship without the efforts in previous seasons of Steve

Davis. He, the club and the supporters, have come a long way together. As the crowd sang to Steve on his final appearance at Turf Moor, "You'll always be a Claret!"

Jerry DAWSON

1907-28

Goalkeeper
522 league games

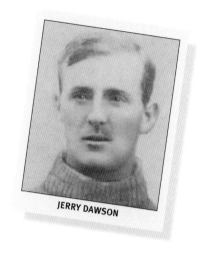

JERRY DAWSON

He had the longest career of any Burnley player. He helped to win the FA Cup. He was in the League Championship team. He played for England. He played more games than anyone ever did for Burnley. Not much else he could have done really!

Of course, we're talking about Jerry Dawson, and we could well add "the legendary" Jerry Dawson. Born in nearby Cliviger in 1888, Jerry was employed as a blacksmith's striker, and his first wages for Burnley were 7/6d per week! He first played for Burnley in 1907 against Stockport. "Dawson, the Reserve goalkeeper, who was given a chance in a League match for the first time, had no opportunity of showing what mettle he is made of. He only handled the ball once, and hadn't really a single shot to stop." So said the local press, which was to write many thousands of words more about him in the years that followed. The team that day read: Dawson; Barron, Moffat; Cretney, McFarlane, Dixon; Whiteley, Whittaker, Ogden, Bell, Smith (A) And Jerry kept a clean sheet!

That was near the end of 1906-07, but only five games into the next season, Jerry had arrived in the first team to stay. During the next 15 seasons, 42 reserve goalkeepers were to come and go, whilst Jerry retained his first team position. We gain a glimpse of Jerry Dawson from the match report of Burnley v Leeds City in 1908: "Five minutes from the end, with the score one all, McLean of Burnley gave a penalty. Bowman took the shot and lifted the ball up to the right of Dawson. But Jerry was prepared, and lame though he was (he had been off the field twenty minutes earlier), he jumped for it, and kept the ball out of the net. McLean gave it a kick, and then Ogden got it away altogether. And then some of the Burnley players ran to Dawson and hung round his neck." (*Burnley Express*)

Burnley were very much in the doldrums when Jerry first signed on, but after him came numerous other names who together were to make the club great. He had his ups and downs did Jerry, witness two incidents from the times: "Dawson missed the train, and Moffat the captain went in goal!" (1910): and "Bradshaw took the free kick at once. So quickly in fact, that Dawson who was hitching up his pants, found the ball entering the net just above his head, almost before he had time to stretch his hand up!" (1916) And on another time: "It is a somewhat peculiar feature that if Jerry Dawson happens to make a bloomer, the rest of the Burnley team go flop, their hearts sink in their shoes, and everything goes wrong. It was so on Saturday, when Dawson allowed a corner kick to slip through his hands." (1919)

But those "lows" of Jerry's career simply emphasise his consistency for over twenty seasons. "Dawson was at his best, diving low, quick to run out, tipping over the bar" was a typical comment from one match report of 1921. Curiously, just as Jerry had missed the final honour in the 1914 Cup Final, so once again, he was missing the day that Burnley received the League Championship trophy in 1921. He missed the final League match through injury. (He, Billy Watson and Billy Nesbitt were the only three players to play in all thirty of the League games without defeat.)

We could fill this book with tales of Jerry Dawson. Of how he played for the English League against the Scottish League at Ibrox in 1913, and after one of his greatest ever displays, the Scottish crowd carried him off shoulder high, and of how practically single handed Jerry kept the Blackburn Rovers attack at bay in the 1913 Cup Tie. One of the most famous incidents occurred prior to the 1914 FA Cup Final at Crystal Palace, when Jerry having been previously injured met the club's directors the night before the game and voluntarily stood down from the Cup Final team, in order that the club might not have to risk playing an unfit goalkeeper. (The FA had a special medal struck for him afterwards)

In 1921-22 after 15 seasons at Turf Moor, Jerry was chosen to play for England. That same month, he was presented with a gold watch by the club in honour of his making 500 appearances for the Burnley first team.. Two seasons later, he chalked up his 600th appearance! By 1926, he had performed on 700 occasions. And by 1928, he had topped the 800 mark. (And this in a career greatly affected by the World War. He made his final First Division appearance in the game against Liverpool at Turf Moor on Christmas Day, 1928, now in his 22nd season with the club. The team for his final match read: Dawson; McCluggage, Waterfield; Steel, Parkin, Forrest; Bruton, Fitton, Beel, Devine, Page. Some members of that team had not been born when Jerry first appeared in 1907!

His leaving the scene had a great national effect. The Arsenal programme, when Burnley played them the week before said: "Almost a quarter of a century in the highest football speaks itself of the greatest qualities, loyalty, consistency, fitness and courage. He leaves the field this week, a credit to himself, to Burnley, and to the game." And that was an Arsenal supporter saying that!

Martin DOBSON

1967-74, 1979-84

Midfielder
406 league games
63 goals

MARTIN DOBSON

The first time that I heard the name of Martin Dobson was over the radio when the team was announced for the Wolves v Burnley game in September 1967. "Who?" I asked myself as the team was read out: Thomson; Smith, Latcham; O'Neill, Ternent, Bellamy; Morgan, Casper, Dobson, Harris and Coates. In those days, we lived in Cumberland. Visits to Turf Moor were rare and news of the club was sparse. I gleaned most information from national radio, as the Clarets in those days were still a leading club in the nation. This "Dobson" I heard, had signed on the previous month after being released by Bolton.. I feared the worst! What did we want with a cast-off from Second Division Bolton, who were fast heading for Division Three?

Little did I, or anyone at Turf Moor for that matter, realise what or who we were seeing. It was the beginning of a great football career and the start for a very fine Claret. Martin Dobson only appeared 11 times in that first season (in three different positions), but as he gradually established himself in the first team, he became one to watch. He played in 22 league games the next season (five positions) and it wasn't until 1969-70 that he became a first team regular (still performing in three positions!) Maybe it was this versatility that held him back? Maybe it was the fact that the Burnley first team midfield was dotted with the likes of Thomas, Coates and Casper?

The answer that we were to realise in later years, was that Martin Dobson could play anywhere in the team, and perform with equal consistency. It is an amazing fact, that in his two spells at Turf Moor, Martin Dobson performed in 10 different positions, as follows:- No.2 (once), No.3 (once), No. 4 (95 games), No.5 (52 games), No.6 (120 games), No.7 (35 games), No.8 (38 games), No.9 (eight games), No.10 (25 games) and No.11 (12 games)

In a word, Martin was class. He was, despite his many positions, one of the old school, straight from the class of Attwell, Shannon and Adamson. Cool, skilful, and a pleasure to watch. Over the years, some Burnley players have been a good reason for "going on to the match" – McIlroy, Pointer, Elliott, Coates and "Dobbo" were among such players. If the game was poor and the score was bad. at least they gave you something good to watch!

There was something akin to Jimmy Adamson about Martin Dobson, and that is a compliment to them both. (Indeed, both had begun as forwards, and both after a while moved back to midfield positions). In my mind's eye, I can still picture Martin gathering the ball from an opposing forward, breaking out of defence, before scattering a wide ranging pass. There was a gracefulness about him, a style and an elegance that immediately caught the eye. Once seen, never forgotten.

Maybe it was Martin's fault that the Clarets were relegated in

1970-71. Sorry Martin – not really your fault! He was injured, and by the time he returned after a broken leg, Burnley had won just once in 17 matches and were bottom. It was a position they never recovered from, and amazingly, Waldron, Thomas, Coates and Co. were relegated. So much we thought for"The Team of the Seventies". But, from the day he returned to the team, Martin only missed three of the next 151 league games.

He became team captain, and he became indispensable. He scored goals too, often from superb headers. Altogether, by the time he had finished playing with the Clarets, Martin had scored 76 goals. 1972-73, the promotion season found Martin at his goalscoring best. That season, he scored a dozen, and all from a midfield position. By now the team read: Stevenson; Docherty, Newton, Dobson, Waldron; Thomson, Ingham; Casper, Fletcher, Thomas and James. Not only was Martin proving to be a superb midfield player and a regular goalscorer, but that season he blossomed into a fine club captain.

Of course, it couldn't last, and soon in 1974-75, the millionaires known as Everton F.C. moved in with a British record fee of £300,000, which Burnley simply couldn't refuse. By now, Martin Dobson was an established England player, but the speed of the transfer took even Martin by surprise. I sat with him on the day he was transferred to Everton in the Bob Lord Stand, watching the Burnley v Chelsea game, and he seemed sad, and even a little hurt that the club had sold him so readily. The reason of course was that same stand we were sat in! It had become a millstone around the club's neck – some blamed it for the original relegation in 1971.And the new stand had cost money, money that could only be found by selling a major asset. The major asset was Martin Dobson, and for years after that, the stand became known as "The Martin Dobson Stand".

Our local hero was gone, and the club declined in stature. When he returned to Turf Moor in 1979, the club were struggling in Division Two and on the brink of relegation. But for the next five seasons, "Dobbo" rolled back the years and performed with all his old skills and grace. He was the last remaining player still surviving from the 1973 Championship team and his experience naturally made him captain again. But John Bond's arrival in 1984 saw an influx of ex Manchester City players and Martin Dobson became unwanted in the new managers' eyes. (Yet another major reason for Bond's unpopularity at Turf Moor).

Among his many honours, Martin Dobson is still the last player to be chosen for England whilst playing for Burnley. Altogether, he made 495 first team appearances for the club. He left us with so many memories – memories that helped the flame to burn even when the prospects since at Turf Moor have been dark. Thanks for the memories, Martin!

Alex ELDER

1959-67

Full back
271 league games
15 goals

ALEX ELDER

Full backs in the forties and fifties were by tradition, big, strong, and usually loaded with experience – they were old! Look back and remember Wally Barnes (Arsenal), Alf Ramsey (Spurs), George Hardwick (Oldham), Alf Sherwood (Cardiff), George Young (Rangers) – Internationals all. Even here at Burnley, we had Arthur Woodruff (still playing, aged 39!) And amid all these, before the decade was out, Burnley had a pair, the equal of any, who were only 36 years old when you added them both together!

Alex Elder was "nobbut a lad" when he signed on for Burnley in January 1959. Like Jimmy McIlroy he came from Glentoran in Northern Ireland. Indeed, he was only just 18 when he made his league debut for Burnley at Deepdale, against Tom Finney of all people (For younger friends, the two most famed and feared wingers in the land – or world? – were Stan Matthews and Tom Finney). The team that day in September 1959 read: Blacklaw; Angus, Elder; Adamson, Cummings, Miller; Connelly, White, Pointer, Robson and

Pilkington. From that day onwards, young Alex only missed one game in the entire season, when he was chosen to play for Northern Ireland in April. By the end of the season, the names of Angus and Elder were known throughout the country, as Burnley sailed to the League Championship in 1960. It must certainly be said that the full back pair were as vital to the Burnley success as the Adamson-McIlroy midfield duo or the Pointer-Robson goalscoring partnership.

Alex Elder was a ferocious tackler and enjoyed moving forward up the wing with the ball. He possessed an extremely hard shot and during his years at Turf Moor, he scored 17 goals (almost a Burnley record for a full back, but still second to fellow Irishman Andy McCluggage who was a bit of a penalty expert). Talking of penalties, probably the most dramatic moment of the season, other than winning the title, came for Alex Elder, when in the Sixth Round FA Cup Tie against Blackburn, Alex stopped a shot and the ball spun up and hit his arm. The whistle blew and the referee pointed to the spot, adjudging the Burnley defender to have handled the ball. You can still hear those who were there on the day debating as to whether or not it was a penalty. (My opinion was that it certainly was not a penalty, and I was as close to Alex Elder as the referee was!) Sadly, my opinion wasn't asked and Brian Douglas scored from the spot. Incidentally, the Clarets were beating, nay walloping, the Rovers 3-0 at the time with only 15 minutes to go. The final result was 3-3 and we lost the replay! I imagine that Alex Elder must have been close to tears that night.

Alex Elder was the regular left back for the next eight seasons. Blacklaw, Angus and Elder created a club record for the back three when they played in 65 consecutive games as Burnley's defence; the sequence was only broken when Alex had to be absent to play for his country. (Altogether he represented Northern Ireland 34 times whilst he was a Claret.) Actually, Blacklaw, Angus and Elder played approx 260 times together in their Clarets days. Inseparable! And John Angus and Alex Elder played together as a full back duo for even more than that!

But you ask anyone who was there for the most lasting memory of Alex Elder and it will always be "that goal." It was 1965-66. Liverpool had the title sewn up but Burnley and Leeds were vying for runners-up position. The final placing hung on the penultimate match between the two clubs at Turf Moor. "With the score at 0-0,

Burnley captain Elder gathered the ball near the left hand corner flag (Bee Hole End), and from a very narrow angle he lobbed the ball back to goalkeeper Blacklaw. Unfortunately, the goalkeeper had come out of his goal, and from an almost impossible angle, Elder sent the ball soaring over Adam Blacklaw's arms into the far corner of the net. It was a truly amazing goal. It would have been a superb shot from a Leeds player; from the Burnley captain, it was incredible. But it proved to be the winning goal, and as a result Leeds clinched the runners up position in the league."

My grandad swore by Len Smelt and David Taylor as a full back pair; my dad never tired of telling me about George Waterfield and Andy McCluggage. I myself was brought up as a child on Arthur Woodruff and Harold Mather. But if I ever see a finer pair of full backs than the skilful and formidable John Angus and Alex Elder, I shall have to rewrite this book!

Brian FLYNN

1972-77, 1982-84

Midfielder
191 league games
19 goals

BRIAN FLYNN

Players don't come much smaller than Brian Flynn; nor do personalities on the pitch come much bigger. He first came to Burnley from his native Welsh Wales as a Welsh Schoolboy International (Goodness knows how small he was in those days!) And he signed as a professional at Turf Moor on his 17th birthday in October 1972. It was towards 18 months later that Brian made his first team debut in the away match at Arsenal. The Burnley team that day read: Stevenson; Noble, Newton; Dobson, Waldron, Thomson; Nulty, Flynn, Fletcher, Collins, Ingham. Two things were certain that

Burnley, 1977

The glory days were over. The team had been relegated the previous year, and were now very much a mid table Second Division team. In three years, the club would be in Division Three! and many supporters felt that the playing kit didn't help!

day. That Brian Flynn was not only the youngest on the pitch, but he was also the smallest!

He began to establish himself permanently in the first team squad during the following season 1974-75. This was Burnley's second season back at the top, and the Clarets had a good season, finishing tenth in Division One. Yet again, it was one of those seasons when with any consistency in form, the club could well have won the title. They finished just eight points behind Champions, Derby County and this after going for a spell of winning just once in the last 10 matches (shades of 1961-62!!)

It must have been an exciting, if exacting season for the young Flynn boy, who made 25 appearances, actually playing in five different positions – to be exact, inside right, right half, right wing and left half, and even once pairing up with defender Keith Newton, as left back. On four occasions, he was substitute, and to show the depth of the Burnley squad, Brian was already playing for Wales at International level that season. An international, but still on the Burnley bench! (The irony continues in the fact that Brian scored for his country, Wales, before he scored his first goal in the league for Burnley!)

Brian was always a great favourite with the Burnley crowd. He was a veritable dynamo, forever on the move, creating chances and making openings from his usual midfield position. 1975-76 was a difficult season both for Brian and Burnley. He played his heart out in the 43 games he played, and in the five different positions he occupied. (And there were still occasions when he was a substitute!) He was the play-anywhere inspiration of the team. He played on the right wing when Willie Morgan was injured; he stood in for Peter Noble in midfield; he replaced the injured Doug Collins and Ray Hankin; and when Leighton James left the club in November, there was Brian deputising on the left wing in a League Cup tie.

For his last season and a half, Brian played in the Number 10 shirt in midfield and displayed great talent. He had immense skills with brilliant ball control, and his size and speed made him a difficult man to mark. And then after 115 first team games, he was gone. He was far too skilled a player to be in the Second Division and Leeds United snapped him up in November 1977 for £175,000.

It was yet another transfer that the Burnley supporters have hated, but which we have had to accept. How we missed him in the next few seasons, and his departure was most certainly a contributing factor to the club's further relegation in 1980. And then wonder of wonders, our hero returned to Turf Moor!

It was now 1982-83 and the season was proving to be one of the most memorable for many a year. It was the season in which we bounced straight down back into the Third Division, but at the same time, took part in two extremely successful cup runs, reaching the Quarter Finals of the FA Cup and the Semi Finals of the League Cup, playing in 16 cup ties altogether that season. Brian Flynn or as he was better known on Turf Moor "The Mighty Flynn" more than played his part in the relegation struggle and the cup runs. The following season, he was almost an ever present as the midfield dynamo, playing in 50 games throughout the season. And in November 1984, he was transferred to Cardiff City, whose crowd must have seen him so often on his many international appearances.

Many players come and go in a lifetime, but some remain forever in your memory. Brian Flynn was one such player. His skill was far greater than his size, and his full hearted efforts and clever ball control endeared him to the Turf Moor crowd forever. In his two periods at Burnley, Brian Flynn played in 243 games and his 33 International caps whilst with the club puts him fourth in Burnley's individual honours, behind McIlroy, Elder and Hamilton. He may have been small in stature, but "Flynny" was one giant of a player!

Bert
FREEMAN

1911-21

Centre forward
166 league games
103 goals

BERT FREEMAN

When Bert Freeman came to Burnley in 1911, he was already a national figure. He had been a top scorer at Arsenal and Everton, he was an English international, and he held the League goal-scoring record with 38 goals in one season for Everton. No wonder then that the headlines in the local press ran: "SENSATIONAL CAPTURE – FREEMAN SECURED FROM EVERTON". The great Bert Freeman made the first of his many appearances with Burnley on April 15th, 1911 in the game against Wolves. The Burnley team that day was: Dawson; Splitt, Bamford; McLaren, Swift, Watson; Morley, Green, Freeman, Mountford, and Mayson. It was in some ways, the beginning of an era. Things began to happen the next season when Bert scored 33 in 34 games! He began like a whirlwind, scoring 19 in his first 17 games. During the season he scored two against both Nottm Forest, and Bristol City, with hat-tricks against Fulham (home and away!) and Glossop.

Inside a season, Bert almost single handed brought the crowds to Turf Moor. From an average of little over 2,000 ten years before, in 1911, Burnley regularly topped 10,000 at Turf Moor and even reached 30,000 in the table topping match against Derby County. ("Of whom were an unprecedented number of ladies" said the local press.) And even though the club failed at the last hurdle to win promotion, Bert Freeman, (once again the league's top scorer), and Burnley Football Club, had warned the country just what to expect. By this time, Everton were already regretting their loss, and I came across this limerick in an Everton programme of the day:-

"We once had a centre called Bert,
Who was constantly on the alert.
When a back mulled the ball,
Play 'The Dead March from Saul',
It's a goal. That's an absolute cert!"

There was a story rife at the time that the *"Liverpool Echo"* paid the club to telegraph the paper every time Bert scored for Burnley! (Was this a Liverpool FC plot?)

The next season, 1912-13 saw local expectations fulfilled. In one game against Leicester Fosse, Bert Freeman scored four out of five, and in the same spell he cracked in eleven within six matches. By Christmas the team from the banks of the Brun were points clear at the top of Division Two, and promotion was achieved in April with games to spare. In winning promotion, Burnley scored a record 88 goals, a club record until they changed the offside law in the 1920's. Of these, Bert Freeman scored 36 in total; for the second season running he was the league's leading scorer and he was the only player in the country to have scored over thirty goals in two consecutive seasons. It is perhaps facts like those which used to make people like my grandad often dwell on "the good old days!"

Bert Freeman was more than a goalscorer – he was not of the ilk of other centre forwards like "Joe Andy" who scored through fearsome, brute force. Bert was a skilled player, with wonderful control, speed and judgement. The local paper said: "Rarely if ever does Freeman do a dirty action. Rather, does he take buffetings calmly, and seldom does he object against the decisions of a referee."

In the 10 years that Bert Freeman was at Burnley (1911-21), his name was every bit as big as any footballer who has ever played – whether it be Matthews and Finney in the fifties Moore or Charlton in the 1960's or Beckham and Rooney in the 21st Century. Just for a glimpse of the Freeman magic, listen to the *"Burnley Express"* in January 1912, writing about the Burnley v Glossop game: "Freeman got to work on the left wing, and after appearing to slip, recovered possession, and sending in from the corner flag, scored a magnificent goal, the ball going into the far corner of the net, from a very narrow angle. It was one of the finest goals ever seen at the ground, and richly deserved the applause it merited." Said the *"Daily Citizen"* in 1913: "Freeman is more like the rapier than the broad sword. You watch him for 10 minutes and perhaps you say: "Freeman has done nothing." And suddenly he is galvanised into life. He traps the ball, he swerves, he dribbles, so that one could imagine that the ball was tied to his boots!" Never was any player more hacked and knocked about, but never did anyone retaliate less; no wonder he was generally known throughout football as "Gentleman Bert".

And so to 1913-14, when newly promoted Burnley were capturing all headlines, especially in the F.A.Cup, where they reached the Final at Crystal Palace. Fourteen excursion trains travelled down to London from Burnley after work on the Friday evening before the game. Around 15,000 Burnley people (including my grandad!) were on those trains (return fare 12 shillings!) as the largest crowd ever to watch a Burnley team in their 32 year history, over 70,000 including the King for the first time, gathered at Crystal Palace.

There was no score until 13 minutes after the interval. "From a throw in on the right, Nesbitt banged the ball across to Hodgson, who had to compete with Longworth. It was a great leap that Hodgson made before he reached the ball above the head of Longworth, but he managed to get his head to the ball, and directed it across to Freeman. Like a flash, the Burnley centre was on the ball, and he snapped up the opportunity without hesitation. Campbell in the Liverpool goal had no chance of saving, and Freeman was almost overwhelmed by the exuberance of the Burnley team who swarmed around him." *(Burnley Gazette)*

And so it was that Burnley brought the F.A.Cup back to the town for the only time, thanks very much to that Bert Freeman goal, as famous as any goal ever scored by a Burnley player. Of course, he scored many more, 115 altogether for Burnley. Illustrations of his talent are too numerous to mention, but let this suffice: "One of Freeman's dribbles with a goal at the end of it is worth going a long way to see, and he trotted one out on Saturday. He ran the ball a third of the length of the field, was challenged by Mitton and Carnpey, eluded them, drew out Cornthwaite, and scored. The shout was almost reminiscent of pre-war days." (Burnley v Bury 1917-18)

When Bert Freeman announced his retirement in 1921, the *"Burnley Express"* said: "No player has been more faithful to the club, nor has the Burnley club ever been better served by a player. No-one who saw him in his prime will ever forget his inimitable style, his lightning darts, and his twinkling feet, as he hung over the ball, controlling it wonderfully. There never was a more gentlemanly player and truly it can be said that Bert Freeman was an example to all who step onto a football field. His name will live in football as long as the game continues because he was one of those who elevated the game. When he came to Burnley from Everton in 1911, the Everton directors said he was finished, but never were men more deceived! Having players of the calibre of Lindley on his left and Kelly on his right. he quickly showed the football world what a force he still was."

When a friend of mine bought a copy of *"Up the Clarets"* for his old next door neighbour, Mrs. Bert Freeman, then living in Birmingham, I took it off him, paid for the book myself, and sent it to the lady, with my own inscription: *"In memory of one of the greatest players who ever wore a Claret jersey!"*

George
HALLEY

1913-22

Wing half
137 league games
4 goals

GEORGE HALLEY

George Halley came to Turf Moor in March 1913. When he arrived, he was the last cog in the machine. Burnley were ready to roll! And when he first played for Burnley on 15 March 1913, local history took a new turn. The team that day against Bury at Turf Moor read: Sewell,

Bamford, Jones; Halley, Boyle, Watson; Mosscrop, Lindley, Freeman, Hodgson, Mountford. And "Halley, Boyle 'n' Watson" were born!

George Halley, a Scot, was a hard but clever player. He was a skilful player with excellent passing qualities. In many way, he complemented his partners, Tommy Boyle and Billy Watson. Boyle was hard and a strong tackler and a leader of men, whilst Watson was an attacking half back who enjoyed his forays up front.

The season that George Halley arrived, the club won promotion. Indeed, it may have just been George's arrival that clinched promotion. In the eight games he played at the end of the season, the team only lost one game.

But it was the following season that history was made locally and nationally, when the club won the F.A.Cup. In the League, George played in 33 of the 38 league games, and en route to the Final, "Halley, Boyle 'n' Watson" played in all eight matches. Having won the Cup, George Halley was one of the first Burnley players to volunteer for the forces, travelling to India and Mesopotamia. It wasn't until 1919 that Turf Moor saw him again.

We must pause to consider what that team of 1914 might have achieved but for the outbreak of war. In 1914 they won the Cup; in 1915, they finished fourth in the league. In 1920, they were second, 1921 saw them champions and 1922 they finished third. That record was only paralleled in 1959-63 when the club finished 1st, 4th, 2nd and 3rd, and a Cup Final appearance.

George Halley was a versatile defender and midfielder, playing left back as well as all three half back roles during his time at Turf Moor. Undoubtedly, his best season was 1920-21, though this was dogged with injury and a severe bout of pneumonia. Despite their lasting fame, it is surprising to learn that the famous trio "Halley, Boyle 'n' Watson" only played together just 115 games. Another fact, hard to realise, is the physical size of these men. None were six footers, or anywhere near that mark. Halley was 5'8" weight 10st 10 lb; Boyle measured 5'6" weight 11st 3 lb, and Watson stood 5'7" weighing 11st 13lb.

It is surely wrong to take any of these three away from the others and compliment or criticise. They were the complete half back line, one of the greatest half back lines that ever played football, and we're not just talking about Turf Moor either! "Halley, Boyle 'n' Watson" rank with the greatest in any generation, Busby, Cowan and Bray

(Manchester City in the 30's), Scoular, Froggatt and Dickinson (Portsmouth in the 50's) or Blanchflower, Norman and McKay (Spurs in the 60's). Billy Meredith, one of the all-time greats, writing in 1921, called them "the sound old plodders". "I doubt" he said, "if one of them could do the 100 yards in 14 seconds. They use their brains more often than they use their feet." My grandad worshipped them, my dad grew up weaned on them. And I wonder how many Burnley fans since, have longed for the likes of those "sound old plodders" since 1922 when they last played together?

During his time at Turf Moor, George Halley played for the "Anglo Scots", and was chosen for the full Scottish international team against Ireland in February 1921, but missed out because he was down with pneumonia. He had a good season in 1921-22, playing more league games than either Tommy Boyle or Billy Watson. But after a dispute with the club over wages, he left Turf Moor in 1922, leaving his name to go down in history. "Halley, Boyle 'n' Watson" – legends!

Jack HILL

1923-28

Wing half
184 league games
13 goals

JACK HILL

Here at Turf Moor, we have supplied the England team with many of our players, but this man was the captain of the England team. And yet if we had to choose a Burnley team from all the pre-war players, the half back line must surely be "Halley, Boyle 'n' Watson." And so Jack Hill, captain of England might only figure as reserve! It only proves the strength of Burnley's half backs down the years.

Big Jack Hill, all 6' 3" of him and weighing 12 stone 12 pounds, came to Burnley from Plymouth Argyle just prior to the 1923-24 season. He arrived at Turf Moor as the result of a record transfer fee, and five years later, when he left Burnley to go to Newcastle, it was for another record fee. In between times, Jack Hill was perhaps the best known player in Britain, as he captained the national team. During that time, he dominated the Burnley defence and inspired the whole Burnley team by his powerful performances. He was at least five and sometimes eight inches taller than any other Burnley defender of his day, and his height and sheer power made him a commanding captain, whom the Turf Moor crowd idolised. Said a local paper on his departure in 1928: "Hill's great size and reach gave him a speed and a strength which were quite unequalled in his day."

His signing for Burnley in 1923 shook the football world, accompanied as it was with the highest fee of the times, around £5,000. After a decade at the top, the club were beginning to struggle when big Jack was signed. The previous season had seen them finish in their lowest Division One position since 1900 when they had been relegated! (Fortunately in 1922-23, the league had more clubs!) He made headlines in his first game – "HILL MAKES SATISFACTORY DEBUT" and the team against Notts County in August 1923 lined up: Dawson; Smelt, Taylor; Watson, Hill, Emerson; Bennie, Kelly, Beel, Cross, Weaver. And then in his second game, Jack scored against Everton.

The position in the League didn't improve in 1923-24, as the club with Jack Hill an ever present, except when he was away on international duty, finished a disappointing seventeenth. But they did reach the FA Cup Semi Final, and big Jack was part of the team that faced Huddersfield Town in the Third Round tie which attracted the highest gate of all time to Turf Moor, some 54,775 (including my dad!) It was one of the most thrilling Cup Ties ever witnessed at Turf Moor as Burnley (who were in the bottom six) beat Huddersfield (who were in the top six) 1-0. Jack Hill, my father never tired of telling me, simply dominated the game. And incidentally, one spectator, James Dodd, aged 69, was killed in the great crush of the crowd. And for younger readers, that season Huddersfield won the League Championship and went on to win it for three consecutive seasons. It could be that Burnley robbed them of "The Double" that season.

There was a cartoon in the *Burnley Express* as the next season started in August 1924. The caption simply read : "There are few changes in the Burnley team – Kelly still wears the longest trousers

– and Hill, the longest legs!" Sadly big Jack missed 17 games that season through injury and surely this was a major reason for Burnley's slump to 19th position? These were the years when First Division Burnley contained England's two finest players, captain Hill and inside forward Bob Kelly. For a few games in 1925, Jack Hill was chosen as right half at Turf Moor, and so successful was he there, that he was chosen for England in that position, along with Bob Kelly in front of him.

The big talking point at the start of the 1925-26 season was the change in the offside rule. Burnley tried it out in a public practice match and Bob Kelly opened up the opposing defence so much that local opinion turned against the new rule. "Who wants to see one team win 20-0?" asked the *"Burnley News"*. Well, in the opening game of the season, the crowd at Villa Park nearly did see such a score. Burnley were the visitors and Capewell scored for the Villa within 30 seconds. Jack Hill became injured and was off the field for most of the game (remember no subs then!) Capewell scored his hat-trick before halftime, and Villa went on to win 10-0. "It could have been twenty" said one Villa player after the match. The Burnley team in that historic game was: Dawson; McCluggage and Waterfield; Basnett, Hill and Parkin; Kelly, Freeman, Roberts, Beel and Page. The team took some real trouncings that season, letting in six three times and eight on two other occasions. In the 8-1 defeat against Bury, goalkeeper Hampson was injured early on, so captain Hill took over in goal and even saved a penalty! And when Rovers beat the Clarets 6-3, again big Jack was absent as he was playing for the English League.

By 1926-27 the Burnley half back line had changed to Steel, Hill and Dougall and was as classy as any since Halley, Boyle 'n' Watson ten years earlier. In one game against Bolton, Burnley goalkeeper George Sommerville broke his collar bone and once again big Jack deputised in goal. This time, he didn't save a penalty, and the team went down 7-1! In November 1927, Turf Moor had a debut of its own when England played Wales at the ground. 32,089 people came to see Burnley's only International game ever. There was very much a Burnley flavour about the occasion as Burnley President Charles E. Sutcliffe was in charge of the team, Burnley trainer, Charlie Bates was the England trainer, and big Jack Hill was the England captain. Sadly, he chose this auspicious occasion to put through his own goal!

The duels in those days between the England captain Hill and opposing centre forwards like Everton's Dixie Dean and Newcastle's Hughie Gallagher were almost national events. No radio, no TV, just newspapers, but they conveyed the enthusiasm of football fans across the land. In August 1928 when Burnley journeyed up to the North East to meet Newcastle, the latest duel was eagerly anticipated. This time it was Jack Hill's day, for Burnley ran riot and were 6-2 ahead by half time! The game ended 7-2 in Burnley's favour, with Hill controlling the midfield like a colossus.

However, it seemed Hill had played too well, and six weeks later, he was a Newcastle player. The Burnley club broke the British transfer record once again. In 1925, it was Bob Kelly who went to Sunderland for £6,550. In 1928, it was Jack Hill who went to Newcastle United for £8,000. It was to be a long time before Burnley saw their like again. Without their captain who had kept them up for six seasons, Burnley were relegated the following season. And it took them 17 seasons to get back in the First Division.

Once again, we have the history of Burnley encapsulated in one player – Crabtree, Kelly, Hill, Bruton, McIlroy, Coates, Dobson. We are told that the club has to sell, and so our hero's leave. And the struggle to survive goes on. My grandad heard it, my dad did, I have heard it, and my son has seen Little, Blake and Chaplow leave. To be continued …

Jack HILLMAN

1891-95, 1898-1902

Goalkeeper
175 league games

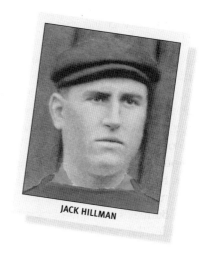

JACK HILLMAN

My grandad used to take me to a shop on a side street just off Leyland Road in Burnley. And we would stand there looking in the shop window. We never went in, but just looked in the window. And there in the window was a football. An old football, painted in blue and white. I had never seen a painted football before and it fascinated me. I went back time and time again to gaze at that old ball .It had a small card against it which read: "This is the football used in the F.A.Cup Final of 1904" I didn't realise at the time that it was painted in Manchester City's colours because that year they won the Cup, with the team; Hillman; McMahon, Burgess; Frost, Hinds, Ashworth; Meredith, Livingstone, Gillespie, Turnbull and Booth. And yes, for those who have heard of him, that was the great Billy Meredith playing on the right wing, and he scored the winning goal that day.

But in goal that day for City was Jack Hillman, and my grandad used to tell me that Jack Hillman owned the shop just off Leyland Road. It didn't mean much to me in those days, but it certainly meant a great deal to my grandad who had seen Jack Hillman hundreds of times. They even lived near each other a hundred years ago! And if only. If only, I had gone in that shop. Just once. And then, I too could have said "I once met Jack Hillman". But hindsight is a wonderful thing!

Jack Hillman came to Burnley as a child and signed for Burnley in 1891, aged 21.He was over six feet tall and weighed well over 16 stone. Large goalkeepers were in vogue in those days, witness "Fatty" Foulke who played for Sheffield United at the same time. Well, Jack Hillman was of that ilk. In Burnley he was popularly known as "the burly one".

The first game he played in the Burnley first team was in September 1891 and Burnley were away at Accrington. The Burnley team was: Hillman; Jeffrey, Lang; McFetteridge, Spiers, Stewart; Bowes, McLardie, Nicol, Graham and Hill. Now before we go any further, we need to learn a little about the times. The same year as Jack Hillman made his debut, goal-nets were first used. Soon afterwards in the same year, the penalty kick was introduced. (To begin with goalkeepers could stand within six yards of the penalty taker – it was only in 1905 that they had to stay on their goal line). Most interesting of all, it was only in 1912 that goalkeepers were restricted to using their hands only in the penalty area. Until then, they could handle the ball anywhere at all – in their own half. Indeed, the original reason for the halfway line was to limit the goalkeepers area of handling. In his own half, he was defending and so he could handle. In the opponents half, he was in the attacking area, where no goalkeeper was expected to be – if he was a *goal* keeper. So, people like Jack Hillman and Jerry Dawson could handle the ball outside the area and anywhere in their own half. It wasn't as easy as it seems because charging was accepted anywhere, and it is little wonder that goalkeepers had to be big and heavy to withstand such robust play. One of the first mentions that Jack Hillman had in the local press was in November 1894: "On Saturday morning, rumours were afloat respecting Hillman's inability to take charge of the sticks, and these proved to be well founded. It transpired that the burly one had been seized with illness during the night, the cause being attributed to his eating mussels for tea."

One wonders what Jack would have made of today's crowds with their mass singing and bawdy chants? We can read what he thought of yesterday's crowds in this report from the Burnley v Bury game in 1894.:"Hillman delayed the start a few minutes, and on coming onto the field, made use of a very offensive expression in reply to a spectator, and this has been much commented on. Such conduct can have only one result, that of alienating a great number of honest admirers of his prowess. I am sorry that Hillman so far forgot himself."

Jack Hillman played for Burnley from 1891 until 1895, rarely missing a game (except when he had eaten mussels!). The Football League had just begun in 1888, and Jack was playing in only its fourth season. In those four seasons at Turf Moor, Jack played in 100 league games. When Jack left Turf Moor in 1895, Burnley were relegated. He spent some months at Everton and then he was transferred to Dundee in what was a sensational transfer at the time. He always claimed that he was the first English professional footballer to be transferred to Scotland. Until then, hundreds of Scots had come in the opposite direction. (At one time, Burnley had 64 on their books and 10 in the first team!) Typical of Hillman's approach to the game and life itself is the story told of his arrival in Scotland. He told the Dundee directors:"My terms, gentlemen, are £50 down and £4 per week. Ye can take 'em or leave 'em, but I don't budge a penny!"One committee member is reported to have said: "Give him what he wants. He will be a great draw, and you will probably find that he is the cheapest man you've got at the finish!"After all this, in the first game he played, Dundee lost 5-0! But later, "Big Jack" became the inspiration of the team, so much so that great crowds turned up wherever Dundee played, simply to watch "the burly one".

At the end of the 1897-98 season, Dundee loaned Jack Hillman back to Burnley for £75, so that he could play for his old team in the last six weeks of the English season. His arrival helped to clinch promotion, and in 1899 he played for the North v the South in the International trial, and then later for the England team against Ireland. He was suspended for the 1900-01 season after he had been found guilty of trying to bribe the Nottm Forest team, though he always laughed off the accusation. In 1902, "Big Jack" left Burnley for £300 and went to Manchester City, where he won a Cup Winners medal and gained promotion in the classic team that included Billy Meredith. A little known fact about Jack Hillman is that he once rescued a woman from drowning in the Burnley canal on 4 June 1906, and then two days later he dived in again at the same spot to save the life of a little boy.

Many thousands of his old fans were delighted when in 1908, aged 37, he came back to Burnley, and for many seasons, he played in the Reserves, with Jerry Dawson in the first team. In 1913, he became assistant trainer to Charlie Bates, but still from time to time, he donned his boots for the club. Even during the Great War, when he was in his late forties, Jack Hillman turned out several times for the first team, and in 1919-20, when Ronnie Sewell refused to play for the Reserves, there was "Big Jack" filling the bill, nearly thirty years after he had first played for Burnley!

Jack Hillman reached the age of 50 in 1921, and the club gave this fine servant, player and trainer, who had also made his name locally as a bowler, cricketer and golfer, a celebration dinner at the Empress Hotel in Burnley. Typical of this gusty personality, was the way in which he stood up after the meal, and entertained the assembled company with a few choice songs! His last recorded appearance for a Burnley team was at the end of the 1920-21 season, when Tommy Boyle took a Burnley team to Manchester to play a game against a selected Manchester team in aid of charities. Jack Hillman played in that game, now aged 50, and he even missed a penalty!

Burnley players and personalities didn't come any bigger than "the burly one!" I just wish that I had gone in that shop!

Jimmy HOGAN

1903-04

Inside forward
50 league games
12 goals

JIMMY HOGAN

I haven't checked, but of all the Burnley players spoken of in this book, Jimmy Hogan probably played the least – just 50 games for the first team. (Now I have checked and Jimmy played twice as many games for Burnley as did Tommy Lawton. And I couldn't miss out Tommy Lawton – could I?) So why is Jimmy Hogan included, when admittedly other players with well over 200 appearances to their name have had to be excluded due to lack of space?

Simply for much the same reason as Tommy Lawton – for what he became. Tommy changed the face of English football with his centre forward skills. Jimmy Hogan altered the face of world football – forever! But we are racing on.

Jimmy was a lad from Nelson, who grew up in the Roman Catholic Church. (he went to the same school and church as my own dad, St.Mary Magdalenes' at Burnley.) As a young player, his team-mates dubbed him "The Parson". He was brought up playing for St.Bede's College in Manchester and afterwards for his church team of St. Mary's in Burnley. Soon he was playing for Burnley Belvedere and then as an 18 year old for his home town of Nelson.

As an inside right, he was an instant success with Nelson and on his first appearance, he scored the winning goal against Blackburn Rovers Reserves with what he always claimed was one of the best shots of his career. He was on five shillings a week, but nearby Rochdale offered him 15 shillings, so to Rochdale he went. The club was struggling, so within a year, Jimmy was unemployed again. Which is when Burnley came on the scene and offered him the unbelievable sum of two pounds a week – a small fortune to the humble accountant.

He arrived at Turf Moor in September 1903, aged 21. As a young inside right he was in a very weak team, with Burnley just having been re-elected to Division Two the previous season. He played his first game at Bristol City in November 1903, when the team was: Towler; Ross, Dixon; Barron, Walders, Taylor; Crawford, Hogan, Jenkinson, Jackson, Williams. In his first game, the team lost 6-0! In his next game, the team lost 6-2 to Glossop North End. But Jimmy retained his place in the team for all the season, and the next season too.

For Burnley, these were days of struggle, gates of a thousand and less, five consecutive defeats in 1903-04 and seven consecutive defeats the next season! Jimmy was a delightful and skilful inside forward and was often what we would describe today as "the man of the match". In his second season, he scored equalisers against Leicester and Chesterfield, as well as winning goals against Doncaster, Chesterfield, Glossop and even Manchester United!

In later years, it was often suggested that Jimmy was an indifferent player, but whilst at Turf Moor, he played 52 times and scored 12 goals. I've seen far more indifferent players playing for Burnley, doing a lot worse than that! But in 1904, Jimmy Hogan had a dispute over wages with manager Spen Whittaker, who refused to pay him £4 a week, and with the help of previous Burnley manager, Harry Bradshaw, Jimmy left Turf Moor. Bradshaw had been Secretary, Chairman and Manager at Turf Moor, but had moved on to Arsenal and Fulham, where he persuaded Jimmy Hogan to join him.

The skills of Jimmy helped Fulham to win the Southern League Championship in 1906 and 1907, and to reach the FA Cup Semi Final in 1908. Sadly, a knee injury almost brought Jimmy Hogan's playing career to a fairly abrupt end. But that was not quite the end of Jimmy as a player. He was signed by Bolton for £600, when the British record was just £1,000. Which suggests again, that Jimmy was far more than an indifferent player. With the Wanderers, he scored 18 goals and helped the club to the Second Division Championship.

His time at Bolton gave him the opportunity to travel with the club and his first trip took him and the club to Holland. Ever since he had been a boy in Nelson, Jimmy Hogan had had an interest in coaching and tactics, and in 1910, Jimmy became the youngest ever

British coach when he went to coach in Holland, where he had previously played on the Bolton tour.

From there, 1912 saw Jimmy go to Austria, where he coached the 1912 Olympic team. And thus began his life of coaching and training, a life which surpassed anything of its like, before or since. He was taken a prisoner of war in Austria, which ended up by him being deported to Hungary. There he coached young footballers. Then later to Switzerland. And Germany. Then to France. Back to Switzerland. England, Scotland, etc, etc. All the time, training, coaching and teaching.

Everyone in the football world has acknowledged the true greatness of Jimmy Hogan, from Len Shackleton to Ferenc Puskas, from Matt Busby to Helmut Schoen, the German coach. When Puskas led the 1953 Hungarians to victory at Wembley, he said: "We owe it all to Jimmy Hogan!" And he was a Burnley lad – the best in the world! Naturally!

Willie IRVINE

1960-68

Centre forward
124 league games
78 goals

WILLIE IRVINE

As a small boy, I lived in Belfast, when my father was in the R.A.F. over there. And so it is part of my make-up that I have often had more than the average Burnley fans support for the likes of Jimmy Mac, Alex Elder, Sammy Todd and Co. And Willie Irvine did nothing to disturb my love for Northern Ireland.

Willie crossed the Irish Sea in 1960, aged 17, and after coming up through the "A" and "B" teams, he appeared in the Reserves in 1961. In those days, regular crowds of 10,000 plus watched the Reserves and believe me, they were well worth watching! In the early 60s, future internationals like Andy Lochhead, Willie Morgan and Willie Irvine were among those who entertained the Turf Moor Reserve regulars – current stars like Pointer, Robson and Connelly were still ruling the roost in the first team. Their play was often staggering, as they scored freely, winning Central League titles and the Lancashire Senior Cup. Personally, I marvelled at young Morgan and Irvine, and despite my idolatry of the first team, I often feared for their future with such Reserves waiting in the wings.

One Saturday in perhaps 62-63, I persuaded my dad to come with me to watch these players. He came as much to please me as anything, but he left Turf Moor that day amazed at what he saw. I think it was Barnsley Reserves that we played that afternoon, and the score was seven or even eight or nine for the Clarets. Willie Irvine scored at least four, maybe five, or was it six? I know memory plays tricks, but we all lost count towards the end! All afternoon, it was a case of watching Willie Morgan (a cross between Matthews and Douglas) beating man after man and crossing the ball to the other Willie who seemed to score one out of every five centres! Ah, memories!

By now (February 1963), Willie had already been chosen to play for the Irish Under 23's team against Wales, and then two months later, he was given his first full Irish International cap when he played against Wales in Belfast. All this before he was 20, and before he played in the Burnley first team! His first game for the Clarets was away to Arsenal in the penultimate match of the season away to Arsenal. For the 13th time in 10 seasons, the Clarets beat Arsenal(!) and incidentally in those 10 seasons, we scored 41 goals against the mighty Arsenal! Ah memories! The Burnley team at Highbury that day in May read: Blacklaw; Angus, Elder; Adamson, Talbut, Miller; Connelly, Bellamy, Irvine, Towers, Harris. And on his debut, Willie scored one of the three goals which beat Arsenal 3-2. Three days later, Willie scored his first hat-trick in the home win against Birmingham.

What with Pointer, Robson and Lochhead (all of whom scored a century of goals for Burnley) all vying for the centre forward positions, it was little wonder that young Willie only played in a handful of games in 1963-64. Nevertheless, his best game was at the end of the season when he scored twice in the 7-2 trouncing of old

Burnley, 1967

Willie Irvine, centre row third from left, pictured with the Burnley team shortly before his transfer to Preston North End.

rivals Tottenham at Turf Moor. Willie Irvine was a versatile centre forward, fast, excellent in the air, with a ready shot. And in 1964-65, the Turf Moor crowd took him to their hearts. During that season, the goals began to flow from the boots and heads of Irvine and Lochhead. In 64-65, they scored 49 between them, with Willie leading the way. Willie's peak time was around Christmas, when he scored seven in December. The following season, things got better, with Willie scored 37 goals in all competitions for the Clarets, equalling Jimmy Robson's all-time record in 1960-61. The goals fairly flowed, as Willie scored twice against Blackpool, West Ham and Sheffield Wednesday, with hat-tricks against Northampton, Nottm Forest and Fulham. He had a run of 10 goals in seven games in the autumn, and another sequence of nine goals in six games in the spring. Truly, a man for all seasons!

But surely, Willie's greatest game that season was in the FA Cup Third Round tie? For the fourth time in six seasons, the draw paired Burnley and Spurs, this time at White Hart Lane. In front of over 50,000, Willie sent Burnley's hopes soaring by scoring in the first 40 seconds. And it seemed unbelievable for those of us there when he scored a second after only four minutes. Spurs fought back to get on level terms with two goals from Alan Gilzean, before Willie put the Clarets on top once more by completing his hat-trick. However, there were signs of relief for Spurs, when with 20 minutes left, they equalised for the second time. And Burnley and Willie Irvine, in particular, had every reason to feel cheated when Gilzean scored the winner from fully 20 yards, just two minutes before the final whistle!

All continued to go well for young Willie Irvine with the goals and the Irish caps continuing to come his way. Until the FA Cup replay at Everton, when after scoring for the Clarets, he broke his leg. The injury meant that he missed the rest of the season, and though he reappeared in 1967-68, somehow his earlier flair in front of goal was not the same. Later that season, he was transferred to Preston, still aged only 25.

But we who were fortunate to see Willie Irvine in his prime are left with a host of good memories. Though he only played in 144 games, he scored 97 goals for the Clarets, and his 17 Irish caps maintained the high proportion of honours that the Burnley-Irish have brought upon themselves and the club. And the partnership of Irvine and Lochhead remains second only in our hearts and in the club records to the post war record of Ray Pointer and Jimmy Robson. Thanks for the memories, Willie!

Leighton JAMES

1970-75, 1978-80, 1986-89

Winger
331 league games
66 goals

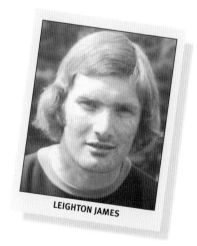

LEIGHTON JAMES

To those who grew up watching Burnley in the 1970's, Leighton James was a god! He was only 17 when he made his league debut for the Clarets in November 1970, the season that Burnley were relegated for the first time in 40 years. Though you could hardly blame "Taffy" for that, seeing that his debut marked only the club's second win in 18 games! The Burnley team that beat Nottm Forest 2-1 on Leighton's debut, read: Mellor; Angus, Nulty; Docherty, Waldron, Dobson; Thomas, Coates, Probert, West and James.

It was the following season that Leighton James established himself as a regular first-teamer, when he took over the number 11 jersey from Steve Kindon. He was very fast with superb ball control; he could make the game a nightmare for opposing full backs, and challenge defences by cutting in and shooting with great power. Add to these natural skills, a fiery Welsh fervour, and there you had "Taffy". To the older generation, he was a reminder of John Connelly at his best, and very soon, he became one of Turf Moor's favourite sons.

In his first game of the new season, "Taffy" scored both goals in the 2-0 away win at Fulham. The following month, he won his first Welsh cap, still aged 18. By doing this, he became the youngest Burnley player ever to win an international cap, beating Messrs Elder and Irvine. But though he was virtually an ever-present after that in 71-72, the season was simply a finding their feet exercise, in preparation for what was to come.

1972-73 had really begun at the end of the previous season with six successive victories. The new season began with a further 16 unbeaten games, making it a run of 22 consecutive unbeaten matches. Leighton played in all these games, and by now he was as famous in the land as any Burnley player. In the middle of this successful sequence, I took my wife to watch Burnley for the first time! There were well over a thousand Burnley fans who made the trip to Hillsborough that day to see the top scoring League leaders, Sheffield Wednesday, play the only unbeaten team in the Football League – Burnley. It was in the eyes of many supporters, the performance of the season as the Clarets gained a splendid 1-0 victory, with a Leighton James special that eventually became one of the goals of the season on TV.

1972-73 was a great season both for Leighton and the Clarets; a further six Welsh caps (curiously, four of them won on the right wing!), an ever-present in the Burnley first team, 10 goals, and promotion! The following season, 1973-74, back in Division One, was much of the same – more caps, more goals and the best season at Turf Moor for eight years, which included an FA Cup Semi Final against Newcastle..

And so "Taffy's" spectacular career continued and it seemed that nothing could stop Burnley's exceptional left winger. By 1974-75, Leighton had only missed two games (through injury) in three seasons. That season he was top scorer for the Clarets, with 17 goals in total, whilst his Welsh international career made him one of the most respected wingers in Europe. Only one thing it seemed, stood in his way – the Clarets weren't winning anything! These days, they would be seen as a well established Premiership club, but in the 70's, success was everything; today, survival is more important.

And so, it seems, in a search for success, "Taffy" left Turf Moor in November 1975, when he moved to League Champions Derby County for £300.000. After short spells at Derby and then with Q.P.R., "Taffy" was back at Turf Moor in September 1978 for a cost of £165,000. He was still a player to catch the eye, but somehow, some of the initial flair had gone, and Leighton only stayed with the club for two seasons. In his second spell at Turf Moor, when Burnley were now a struggling Second Division outfit, Leighton only scored nine goals in 76 league games. He finished up playing on the right wing, having lost his number 11 jersey to Malcolm Smith. And the 1979-80 season ended with relegation to the Third Division, and Leighton James leaving Turf Moor for the second time. This time to Swansea City for £130,000.

Then began a tour of clubs which included Swansea, Sunderland, Bury and Newport County, before, amazingly in July 1986, he returned to Turf Moor, to sign for Burnley for the third time! It was July 1986, and on reflection it could have been one of the most important signings in the club's history. Maybe, it was a case of the old saying – "the right man at the right moment".

Little did we or anyone know that 1986-87 would be such a decisive season for the Clarets. Though we should have been prepared, seeing that our beloved team had finished in the bottom half of the Fourth Division the previous season. By now, "Taffy" was more at home in a midfield role, rather than his former fleet of foot wing position. During the season, he played in 42 games and scored some vital goals. He finished as top scorer with 12 goals, including winners against Scunthorpe and Southend. Certainly without his

Leighton James, 1975

Leighton converts a penalty for the Clarets against Derby County's Les Green.

presence and his goals, Burnley would have been relegated weeks before the final dramatic game against Orient.

But there he was, playing in perhaps the most famous game in the club's 100 year history, and playing in a number nine shirt as well. The result of course is history, and "Taffy" and the Clarets lived to play another day. 1987-88 was a season of relief and repair, as the club struggled back to a little respectability, finishing 10th in Division Four. "Taffy" was now a regular midfielder, filling any role where he was needed. And many older Burnley fans felt that it was just reward for his services when he came on the Wembley pitch as substitute in the Sherpa Van Final in May 1988. Some great players never played at Wembley. For "Taffy", it was his 10th game there, both as a Welsh international and a Burnley player.

By the time he played his final game for the Clarets in the last game of the season of 1988-89, Leighton James was by far the senior member of the squad, now aged 36. His Burnley career had seen some of the most dramatic days in the club's history. As a youngster, he saw Burnley relegated in 1971 for the first time since 1930; two seasons later, he was a vital part of the Burnley team winning promotion in 1973; he played when they fought for their lives and the club's future at the bottom of the Fourth Division, and he played for them at Wembley. Altogether, 397 games in a Claret jersey, scoring some memorable goals. As long as football is played at Burnley, the locals will remember "Taffy"

Bob KELLY

1913-25

Inside forward
277 league games
88 goals

BOB KELLY

You could write a book about Bob Kelly. He first came to Turf Moor in November 1913, when he was signed by the club from St. Helen's Town, for £275, said to be the highest fee ever paid for a Lancashire Combination player. One newspaper described the 19 year old Kelly as: "The most talked of player in Lancashire junior football circles – a second Buchan!"

Inside a week, he was in the first team, when regular, Teddy Hodgson was injured, and he scored in the 4-0 trouncing of the Cup holders, Aston Villa. The Burnley papers spoke of "this young man's sensational debut – a born footballer." The team that day in 1913 read: Dawson; Bamford, Jones; Thorpe, Boyle, Watson; Mosscrop, Lindley, Freeman, Kelly and Husband. However, the club had such a depth of fine players that Bob only played in a handful of games that season, always filling in for whoever happened to be injured.

The next season, 1914-15, he arrived! With the outset of war, several players were unavailable, and Bob found first team opportunities more readily available. He started on the right wing replacing Billy Nesbitt, and later moved inside to take the place of Dick Lindley. His contribution was immediate and immense. In 30 games, he scored 12 goals, and he and his forward colleagues of Bert Freeman and Teddy Hodgson, scored 47 goals, as the Clarets recorded their highest Division One position since 1899. His ball control was breathtaking and his eye for an opening was tremendous. The local papers, not prone to exaggeration, regularly printed sensational reports of this 21 year old. "Lindley and Kelly were a magnificent wing". "No one was better on the field than Kelly". "Kelly improves every game he plays"

Because of wartime service, Bob's career was slowed down until 1919, when Burnley mounted their first serious attack on the League Championship. However, their challenge faded when they went from mid December to the start of February without winning a game. Included in this run was the cup tie against Sunderland, when the biggest crowd of the season, some 33,222, saw the Clarets (which they were now being called) draw 1-1 thanks to Bob Kelly's equaliser. It was perhaps typical of the strain of playing in those days, and of the efforts of Bob Kelly, that he had to take to his bed after the match, and was there for several days.

On the day in March 1920, when Joe "Andy" made his Turf Moor debut, Bob Kelly was missing from the team. That day, he was playing for the English League against the Scottish League, his first major honour since coming to Burnley. One national newspaper report read: "Bob Kelly played a brilliant game and appears to have taken over the inside forward position from Buchan." Kelly scored in the English League's 4-1 win. As a result of his spectacular debut, he was chosen for England and Bob played his first international against Scotland at Sheffield in April 1920. England won 5-4 and Bob Kelly scored two of his country's goals! He was unstoppable! "THE GREATNESS OF KELLY" was the headlines in the *"Athletic News"*: "The best forward on the field" was the way that the *"Sunday Chronicle"* described him, whilst the *"Daily News"* reported the following: "England's strength was in attack, all five players were first class, with Kelly touching greatness. The Burnley man has a turn of speed, an elusive swerve, and perfect ball control, and England has not had a better inside forward since Bloomer at his best."

It was now 1920-21 and the scene was set for the Clarets to make history. After an indifferent start, the team hit form, though Bob missed the occasional game due to his international commitments. (He played for England against Ireland at Sunderland and scored one of the two goals that won the game.) By November, the two teams heading the League were Newcastle United and Burnley. That was until the Clarets beat the Geordies twice inside a week! 50,000 saw the 2-1 victory at St.James' Park, with Kelly scoring the winner. The following Saturday, a club record of 38,860 saw Burnley win again, this time 3-1, with Bob scoring another. "AND THAT WAS THE MUCH VAUNTED NEWCASTLE TEAM" ran the headlines after the match. That was the team's sixth successive victory and it was now 11 games without defeat.

A fortnight later when Oldham came to Turf Moor, Burnley were established as league leaders. By this time, Burnley were the talk of every pub and club in the land and Bob Kelly was the toast of the nation. Wherever they went, vast crowds turned out to see the Clarets with their young genius, Bob Kelly. On 30 occasions that season, the crowds topped 30,000, and at three away games at Newcastle, Sheffield United and Bolton, the figures topped 50,000.

After the Oldham game at Turf Moor, which Burnley won 7-1, the headlines ran: "THE WIZARDRY OF BURNLEY!" Listen to this!: "Not many times in the life of a football spectator is it permitted to watch football such as that of Saturday, which gained Burnley the biggest bag of goals which has fallen to their lot in 19 years. Saturday's display will live in history – not merely for the glut of goals, but for all the glorious football that the team showed. 'I have been following football for 38 years' said a well known Burnley man at the close, 'but I never saw such wonderful football in the whole course of my life, as I saw in the first 15 minutes of the game today.' The play of the Burnley side was too staggering for words. Kelly was surely an inspiration to see, swaying like a reed in the wind, deceiving, feinting, then slipping through the defence on his own, or co-operating with Nesbitt in a manner which brought the pair, cheer after cheer. Theirs was surely the acme of scientific skill" (*Burnley News*). To sum up, Bob Kelly scored four, Benny Cross got a couple and Tommy Boyle added the seventh.

And so it went on – the team scored seven goals in the two games against Sheffield United, another seven in the games against Blackburn Rovers, five in the two games against Preston, and another seven in the Aston Villa matches. Burnley Football Club, now having played 25 games since their last defeat were the topic of conversation in the barber's shop, in the Church vestry, in the smoking room, and on the trams. On Easter Saturday, the team were eventually beaten by Manchester City, 3-0, but came Easter Monday and it was "business as usual" for the Burnley team. They were still in Manchester, but this time at Old Trafford – an Old Trafford ankle deep in mud, to play the United team. "THE REAL BURNLEY AGAIN – THE MAGIC OF KELLY" roared the local papers. Boyle, Anderson, and of course Kelly, were the scorers to give Burnley two more valuable points, but it would be almost sinful to omit the following account which appeared the week after, in the *"Burnley News"*:

"THE MAGIC OF KELLY"

"And so Kelly took matters into his own hands, and thrilled the crowd by his stupendous individualism. Swerving, writhing, wriggling through obstacles, jumping over extended feet, and carrying the ball with him all the time, he electrified the crowd by some of the most magnificent runs it has ever been their lot to see. Not once or twice, but a host of times, he broke away like a fox with the hounds streaming in full cry behind him, and the crowd hugged themselves in ecstasy, and the cry of "He's off again!" could be clearly heard. Wildly fascinated, the crowd waited for these exciting runs. They commenced towards the close of the first half. Just one minute was wanted till half-time, and then Kelly set off again. He worked right away from his own position to the left, dodging and dribbling cleverly, and avoiding the defence till he was well within the penalty area, and an almost certain scorer. And then Silcock kicked his legs from under him. Referee! Spot! BOYLE! Goal!!!"

As mentioned before, newspaper reports in those days were couched in modest, undramatic and somewhat conservative terms. And so, the greatness of both the Burnley team and Bob Kelly should be doubled by the sheer enthusiasm of the reporting. Let the last word about the 30 games without defeat come from a man of the times, "Kestrel", who wrote all the Burnley F.C. articles in the *"Burnley News"*. "So an end has been put to Burnley's record-breaking run. But do we mind? Not a bit of it! We have been partners with the greatest team that ever was. We know full well that never in our time will such a thing be accomplished again, and we like to think that we live in an age that will be remembered when we are personally forgotten." How true you were, Kestrel, old friend! And 25 years later in 1946, I well remember my grandad saying much the same thing, that no matter how long I lived, I would never see such football as he had seen from Burnley and Bob Kelly.

The last match of the season when Burnley received the League Championship trophy was against Sunderland at Turf Moor. The result was 2-2, and Nesbitt and Kelly levelled the scores for Burnley. Said the local paper: "Rarely have Kelly and Nesbitt operated better than on Saturday. Nesbitt had the Sunderland defence in a hopeless tangle, whilst Kelly let himself go thoroughly, and played what is known in football parlance as a "blinder". He dragged the Sunderland defence over half the field with him on many occasions." The last word of that remarkable season comes from the match report on the F.A. Charity Shield game played that May between Tottenham, the Cup Winners, and Burnley, the League Champions. Spurs won 2-1, but the match report includes a paragraph with the familiar heading "KELLY THE WIZARD!" "Kelly of course! There was not another like him. He was a gay spark, full of humour, and often his way of running around the ball, side-stepping and dodging, aroused great peals of laughter and cheers."

Came 1921-22 and Bob Kelly continued on his notable course, playing for England v The North, and England v The South, which were the two international trials. Along with Jerry Dawson, he was chosen for the England team to play Scotland at Villa Park. Indeed, whilst at Turf Moor, Bob Kelly played seven times for the Football League and 11 times (still a club record) for England. There were even suggestions that he was too good for Burnley! "There is no doubt that Kelly is one of the greatest artists in the game. In fact, one is sometimes inclined to think that he is too great an artist for his colleagues, and that his super brilliance does not tend towards a harmonious working of the side." So said the *Burnley News* in 1924.

The big talking point at the start of 1925-26 was the change in the offside rule. Burnley tried it out in a public practice match, and Bob Kelly opened up the opposing defence so much that local opinion turned against the new rule. "Who wants to see one team win 20-0?" asked "Kestrel". In the first league game of the season, Burnley went to Aston Villa and lost 10-0! After only 17 games, Burnley had conceded 50 goals and were bottom of the league. The club were also struggling in deep financial waters too. But worse was to come!

A brief stop press paragraph on the back page of the *Burnley News* of 2 December 1925, created the biggest news of the season, and people were still talking about it 50 years later.

"BOB KELLY TRANSFERRED TO SUNDERLAND"

During the following week, the reports of his departure read like an obituary. "Departure of Kelly". "Blow to Burnley Football Club!". "Never has a greater blow been administered to the Burnley public than the transfer of Bob Kelly". "He was the first player ever to be brought through the Burnley teams, and sold for any amount". "No man has ever been so greatly honoured whilst playing for Burnley". "To those who saw him, the memory of his brilliant play will remain for life, the sinuous moves, his deceptive body swerve, his speed off the mark, the spectacular shot, his ball jugglery, all in all – a football wizard!" Whilst "Kestrel" of the *"Burnley News"* summed up Bob Kelly's departure in his usual prophetic way: "We part with him with regret, fearing that we may never see his like again." Very few players have done anything to make "Kestrel" eat his sad words, since that day in December 1925. The transfer fee was a British record fee, amounting to £6,550.

My uncle who knew a thing or two about football once wrote: "The greatest player who ever laced on a football boot was Bob Kelly. I saw Charlie Buchan and Jimmy McIlroy, I've seen Pele and Eusebio, Matthews and Finney, and a few others whose names escape me, but none of them were in Kelly's class. He had all the ball control and trickery that the others I've named had, he was as brilliant a player, but after that he had something else – he could break a game open. He didn't dribble the ball in the accepted sense, he ran with it. On one of his runs he would beat opponents with speed, with sharp turns, with body movements, and such was his speed that a man once beaten could never catch up with him again in that run. Kelly could leave five or six beaten men and he was in the penalty area before they recovered."

If we ever had the good fortune to pick a "Burnley All Stars" team, Bob Kelly is as obvious a choice as Jerry Dawson, and Halley, Boyle 'n' Watson. Who is there who ever saw Bob Kelly's body swerve who will ever forget it? In one practice match at Turf Moor, ex-player Fred Blinkhorn recalled: "I'll swear to this day that Bob Kelly walked straight through me. I had him blocked in at the corner flag, he couldn't get round me – but he did!" When Kelly left Burnley in 1925., there was as much local outcry as when Matthews left Stoke or when McIlroy left Turf Moor. And with his departure, Burnley were booking their ticket for a struggle which ended in relegation.

I had a good friend called Bill Smith who also knew his football and had seen them all. Kelly was the greatest, he always told me. Bill was Director of Education on the Fylde and 40 years after Bob Kelly had left Turf Moor, Bill was interviewing candidates for a post as school caretaker at a Fylde school. The next man to be interviewed was called Kelly. As the short built man came in, Bill recognised his walk. Bill said "I stood in his presence and asked 'Are you him?' " "I suppose that I am" smiled Bob modestly. And Bill smiled too when he told me that he got the job!

Alex (Sandy) LANG

1885-95

Full back
123 league games
2 goals

ALEX LANG

In the mid 1880's, Scotsmen flooded into Burnley. The main reason was "King Cotton" and the jobs that were available at the mills. The Scots also poured into Burnley F.C., and at one time in 1884 there was only one Englishman in the team. One of those many Scots players was Alexander ("Sandy") Lang.

Sandy had come from Paisley to Padiham in 1884. In those days, Padiham had a much stronger team than Burnley. (In the two games played between the clubs in 1884, Padiham had won 9-1 and 4-2!) No doubt that in those games, Sandy Lang was playing for Padiham. He joined the Turf Moor club as a 21 year old in 1885.

In those pre-League days, the clubs played friendlies and the regular team, playing in the usual colours of blue and white stripes, turned out like this: McLintock; Lang and Sugg; Keenan, Beattie and Abrahams; McNee, McCrae, Friel, Kennedy and Wood. And because they played at Turf Moor, they were nicknamed "The Moorites".

Sandy Lang was playing on the day that Prince Albert, son of Queen Victoria, came to town to open the new Victoria Hospital in Burnley. Part of the Princes' programme was a visit to Turf Moor to watch the Burnley v Bolton Wanderers game, which Bolton won 4-3. Previous to the game, events like the Hospital Cup had played no small part in raising money for the hospital. It is believed that this was the first recorded occasion on which any member of the Royal Family graced a football match, and for many years later, "The Moorites" became known as "The Royalites".

In many ways, Sandy Lang could be described as "the first". He was a member of the first Burnley team ever to play League football when on 8 September 1888, Burnley went to Preston and lost 5-2. The team that represented Burnley that day was a blend of youth and experience: Kay; Bury and Lang; Abrahams, Friel and Keenan; Hibbert, Brady, Poland, Gallocher and Yates. And Sandy Lang, now in his fifth season at Turf Moor was the first club captain.

It was six years later before Sandy lost his first team spot. He was a versatile defender, playing right back, left back and centre half. He was a strong player with a reputation for hard tackling. In those six seasons of hard, physical, robust football where shoulder charging and sliding tackles were the norm, Sandy only missed eight games. Indeed, he was the first Burnley player ever to play a 100 games for the club.

Sandy was playing with left winger Jack Yates, Burnley's first international in 1888; he played with Claude Lambie ("Lambie the Leap", the club's first free scoring centre forward) in 1890; he was there when goalkeeper Jack Hillman made his Burnley debut in 1891; and he played alongside young Crabtree in 1893, the same James Crabtree who would later captain England. All this time, Sandy Lang was the club captain, and the team became nationally known as "Lang's Eleven". Incidentally, Sandy was the first Burnley player ever to score a penalty, when he scored from the spot against West Brom in 1891

In 1889-90, the club had a disastrous season, not winning until their eighteenth game. But they had a fine run in the Lancashire Cup, and in one game against Haydock, they scored 15 goals, with defender Sandy scoring twice himself. In the Final, Burnley met the mighty Blackburn Rovers, then in their seventh Lancashire Cup

Burnley, 1889-90

Probably the oldest photograph of any Burnley Football Club team. 1889-90 was a memorable year for the "Moorites" – they failed to win a league game between between September and March! The trophy was the Lancashire Senior Cup won by the club that season.

Final. But that day a Lancashire Cup record crowd of over 15,000 saw Burnley rise to the occasion with a fine 2-0 victory in the Final at Accrington. "FOR 'TWAS A GLORIOUS VICTORY!" sang out the local newspapers. with headlines like "ROUT OF THE ENGLISH CUP HOLDERS" and "TODAY, BURNLEY FOOTBALL STANDS ON A HIGHER RUNG THAN IT HAS EVER STOOD BEFORE."The *"Athletic News"* said: "I never saw the Blackburn Rovers better beaten than they were in the Lancashire Final on Saturday. Burnley overplayed them in every direction, and one could hardly believe that we had the winners of the English Cup fighting such a hopeless battle." Back in Burnley, "Lang's Eleven" received a rapturous reception from the townspeople, with large crowds gathering at the Mitre, down Westgate, and through St.James' Street into the town centre, cheering the horse drawn coach all the way.

After 10 years at Turf Moor and hundreds of friendly pre-league appearances as well as 123 League games, Sandy Lang played his final game for Burnley in March 1895. Many hundreds of players would follow him, but as team player, club captain, penalty taker and Cup winner, he was the first!

Tommy LAWTON

1935-36

Centre forward
25 league games
16 goals

TOMMY LAWTON

My dad was a bus conductor for the B.C. & N. Joint Transport or "The Tramways" as it used to be known. Like the shopkeeper, which he later became, he knew his regular customers well. And Tommy Lawton was one such passenger on my dad's Brunshaw Road bus. Burnley was a close-knit community, and just as my grandad knew Benny Cross and Billy Watson, and as I later knew Jimmy Robson personally, so my dad befriended the young boy who travelled regularly on his bus called Tommy Lawton. Within a year, the whole of Burnley would know the name, and in the next decade, the world would flock to see him.

Of all the players in this book, none played less games for Burnley as did Tommy Lawton – just 25 in all. But it is likely that none became more famous. So how could we miss him out?

I have a letter from Fred Taylor, whom we must introduce at this moment. In 1934, 15 year old Fred Taylor scored 11 goals for Briercliffe St.James' in a 24-1 victory in the Burnley Sunday School League. He had already scored over 100 goals that season and Burnley signed him on as an amateur. The signing of such a young player was so unusual in those days, that the local papers were full of it. Fred writes: "I was working in the weaving mill in Harle Syke in 1934. I was 14 years old, when Billy Dougall and Ray Bennion came up and asked my Dad if I could go to Burnley on the ground staff. He said "Yes" and so there I was in the office at Turf Moor with Alf Boland. I had been there about three months when a great big strapping lad came to join me in the office. Tommy Lawton had arrived at Burnley. He was a natural, a terrific shot with either foot, a great header, and very fast over twenty five yards.After that, quite a lot of young lads came – Len Martindale, George Knight, and Harry Potts."What Fred was witnessing was the very early days of Burnley's youth policy, which would grow and blossom after the War.

The *"Burnley Express"* reported on 20 February 1935: "In accordance with their policy of judicious building up for the future, Burnley FC have signed another young amateur centre forward. He is Thomas Lawton, a Bolton boy, whose feats in junior football circles have attracted the attention of several League clubs. 15 years of age, he has enjoyed practically all the honours of schoolboy football, having captained his school team, his home town, the Lancashire team, and also had three internaional trials with the England schoolboys.

In the last three seasons, he has scored 520 goals. This promising young player is well endowed physically, standing just over 5'10"and weighing 11st 7lb. About a month ago, he had a run with Rossendale United's Lancashire Combination team, and scored three goals against Leyland Motors. He will probably appear in Burnley's West Lancashire League side on Saturday." (Incidentally, young Tommy did play, and he scored two goals on his debut!)

By May 1935, Tommy Lawton was capturing all the local sports headlines in Burnley, as he continued to catch the eye, playing for the "A"team. In May 1935, the *"Burnley Express"*reported;"A magnificent performance by Lawton, a schoolboy international of exceptional promise, enabled Burnley 'A' to round off a successful season last Saturday. All four goals for the home side were scored by the young centre-forward. Cool, precise, and always on the lookout for loopholes in the Bury defence, Lawton played a scientific game, and it is no exaggeration to say that most of the spectators spent the afternoon watching him alone."

But came the new football season, and the young Lawton was raring to go! The Burnley team were no great shakes in 1935-36 and relegation from Division Two loomed dark on the horizon. Still learning in the 'A' team, Tommy was given a run in the Reserves against Manchester City, still aged only 15! He obviously was having a struggle playing alongside grown men and he only scored three times in 13 games. But, with the first team losing far more games than they were winning, Ray Bennion suggested that young Tommy

Lawton be given a chance in the first team, adding "he can't do any worse!"

It was the beginning of a great career, and my dad was there that day to see his young friend. When Tommy played his first game for Burnley on 28 March 1936, the headlines in the *"Burnley Express"* were "BURNLEY'S BOY LEADER". At the ripe old age of 16 years and 174 days, he was the youngest player ever to play for the Burnley first team. And more than 70 years later, he still is! The Burnley team playing Doncaster Rovers on that memorable occasion at Turf Moor read: Adams; Richmond, Hubbick; Hindmarsh, Johnson, Robinson; Hancock, Brocklebank, Lawton, Hornby and Fletcher. No goals for Tommy that day, but a valuable point was won in the 1-1 draw (it was a month since Burnley had last won! And Burnley were fourth from the bottom with only eight games to play.) Tommy was disappointed with his performance; "I didn't play very well. I was overawed. I thought I'd let everyone down. I cried myself to sleep that night, and thought I'd be better off giving up the game, there was no future for me."

The following Saturday, Burnley were away at Swansea, and won a vital game 3-1. "Midway through the first half, Ronnie Hornby crossed from the left. High above everyone else in the area, Lawton's head made contact with the ball and it bulleted into the back of the net." Tommy said later: "I was mesmerised. Alick Robinson raced across to hug me. Together we dashed over to Ronnie Hornby. I was overjoyed.""In the second half, Robinson from left half, produced the perfect through pass that Lawton ran onto, and right footed, hit the ball powerfully past the goalkeeper for his second."

And so the 1935-36 season came to a close, with Burnley and Tommy winning nine points from their last nine games. Lawton scored five times in the seven games he played, and Burnley escaped relegation by just five points. Would Burnley have gone into the Third Division without the advent of their "boy leader"? We will never know, but he had certainly made a vital difference just at the right time.

Ray Bennion was Tommy Lawton's great coach, trainer and advocate. Years later, Tommy said "He was a hard taskmaster, but I'm glad now that he was.". Now into the cricket season of 1936, Tommy established himself as one of the most spectacular batsmen to play for the Burnley team for many a season. There are many stories retold of how he hit the ball on one occasion over the cricket field stand on the football field, and they found the ball in the centre circle! (West Indian professional Collie Smith was one of just a few others who have achieved this feat) My dad was on the Turf one afternoon, when Tommy hit the ball out of the ground and broke a window in St.Mary's Church across the road! That season Tommy topped the Burnley batting averages – again no small feat for a 16 year old!

The following season, 1936-37 started brightly with Burnley scoring four in their first two games, and Tommy got three of them! Due to injury, Tommy missed five games in September, but in October, he celebrated his 17th birthday. This meant that he could sign professional forms for the club, which he did, the day before the home game against Tottenham. 20,447 came to Turf Moor that day, by far the biggest gate that season, such was the local interest in the young centre forward. And the rest is history!

Within 30 seconds, he had scored with a powerful shot. His second goal was a header at the far post, when he out jumped everyone else in the penalty area. And three minutes into the second half, he cracked in an unstoppable shot for number three. His first league hat-trick, against Tottenham of all teams! Aged 17! It must have been obvious to anyone in Burnley or further afield, that his days at Turf Moor with a debt-riddled Second Division club were numbered. And so it was that in December, he was transferred to First Division Everton. By that time, Tommy had scored 11 goals in his 18 games that season, making a total of 16 goals in the 25 games which made up his Burnley career.

The transfer fee was £6,500, easily a record for a 17 year old. By the time he was 19, Tommy Lawton was an England regular and Everton were Division One Champions. By this time, Tommy Lawton was the best known name in football and his head and hairstyle the most easily recognised in the land. Tommy only returned to Turf Moor once again as a player, and that was 18 years later in February 1955, when he played for Arsenal in the 3-0 defeat by the Clarets. It was the only time I ever saw him play.

P.S. What happened to Tommy's first friend at Turf Moor, Fred Taylor? The season after Tommy Lawton left Burnley, Fred made his league debut on the right wing in the game against Norwich City. "I wouldn't have missed this game for a gold clock" said "Sportsman" of the *"Burnley Express"* afterwards, for Burnley won 3-0, and the 17 year old Fred Taylor scored two of them. However, the war cut short his career, and he left Turf Moor after just 49 league games.

Glen
LITTLE

1996-2004

Midfield
211 league games
32 goals

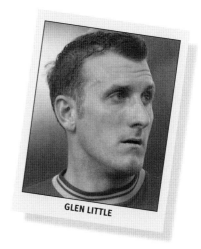

GLEN LITTLE

Out of all the portraits contained in this collection, that of Glen Little is unique, insofar as he is the only one still playing! Glen, a Londoner, arrived in our lives at Turf Moor in 1996-97 from Crystal Palace, via Glentoran (incidentally, some other Burnley players had come from there over the years!)

It was the first League game of 1997 in the away game at Bristol City that Glen made his Clarets debut. That day, the Burnley team read: Russell, Parkinson, Vinnicombe, Harrison, Swan, Brass, Little, Smith, Cooke, Barnes and Gleghorn. However, he flitted in and out of the team, making just five appearances that season; three of these were away games so the average Burnley fan never knew what they were missing! The management having signed him, didn't seem to rate him so highly as Damian Matthew, Paul Weller, and Gerry Harrison all played more games on the right wing than Glen.

The following season, 1997-98 was no different. O.K. different chairman, different manager, but Glen was still in the Reserves. Some have suggested that because Chris Waddle was now the manager and Chris Waddle played on the right wing, then few others including Glen Little would ever get the opportunity to play in the outside right position. So, just five times on the bench and then suddenly – a change of heart! It was the Watford game at home in early January 1998 that Glen re-emerged playing midfield. Curiously though the Clarets were bottom and hadn't won for six games, they did that day! Curiously, Andy Payton made his debut the following week. Curiously after that, Burnley won more of their remaining games than they lost. And most curiously, Burnley having been bottom of Division Two when Glen made his debut in January, escaped relegation in May! It makes you think!!

The change could be seen from the stands, there was a new feeling with Glen Little in the team. Here was a man who could control the ball like few we had seen for some time. He dribbled, he took the ball to the bye-line, he made pin point centres, and the crowd loved it. And him. Very soon, they took up the cry: "Su-u-uper, super Glen" which became a regular anthem for the next few years at Turf Moor.

When the new season of 1998-99 began, the first game was at Turf Moor against Bristol Rovers. The front cover of the programme was a colour photo of Glen – almost a statement of faith! I read that Manchester City were clear favourites to win the Second Division title, we at Turf Moor were fifth favourites along with Northampton. Cautiously optimistic. They were all wrong! In the end, Fulham walked away with the League, City finished third, and Northampton were relegated! The Clarets finished middle(ish) in the League (actually bottom half!) It could have been worse. A lot worse!!

The season began OK with Burnley beating Bristol 2-1 and Glen setting up both goals for Andy Payton. But by the time October came five defeats and four draws later, Burnley and Glen were in the bottom four! Things didn't get much better for either of them. Glen had to undergo a double hernia operation which ruled him out for eight games, and six defeats and three draws later, the Clarets were a very wobbly seventeenth as we entered 1999. As Stan said in his programme notes: "It would be fair to say that the first half of the season has not been what I was either expecting or hoping for."

The crunch came on my 59th birthday, when the Clarets lost 5-0 at home to Gillingham, and then 6-0 in the next match at home to Manchester City. Altogether four games lost on the run, no goals for and 14 against. With 10 games to play, our beloved Clarets were in the bottom four and looking favourites for relegation. And then, just as in the previous season, when Glen and Andy did their rescue act for "The Great Escape", so now they did it again. Of course they were members of the entire team, but let's put it another way – without

Glen Little, 1997-2004

Glen parading the skills that Clarets' fans loved, skipping past a forlorn defender.

Payton and Little at the end of the 98-99 season, the Clarets would surely have been relegated. Eleven games, all unbeaten, six goals from Payton, four from Little, and the whole style of play was rejuvenated.

No team was spared, even League champions Fulham came to Turf Moor and were beaten! Glen Little was superb in that spell, taking on two, three and sometimes four opponents, dribbling in from the corner flag, getting through spaces when there seemed to be no space to get through. And phew, we had escaped again!

Came 1999-2000, and most clubs were favourites to succeed, except Burnley! Not after two nail biting escapes from relegation! Wrong again! That season, the Clarets were never out of the top six, and Glen was the town hero. Of course, there were other heroes that season like Andy Payton and Ian Wright, but for my money, Glen reigned supreme. Burnley fans are still talking about his wonder goal against Bristol Rovers when he seemingly beat man after man after man (after man!) in the penalty area, before putting the ball in the net. He figured in 41 of the club's league games, and the chances and the goals he created were without number. Burnley were once again, after many years, an exciting team to watch, and the crowds came back to Turf Moor. (We even topped 20,000 twice, a figure the ground had only held twice in twenty seasons!) And at the end of it all, thanks to Glen's great winner at Scunthorpe, Burnley were back in Division One. The season's triumph was celebrated with a tour of the town by the players on an open top bus, when Glen had a drop to drink!

The first season after promotion, 2000-01 was a season of "what might have been". It was a good season, bordering on great (after the traumas of Division Two!), and the Clarets finished seventh, just one spot off the Play-Offs. How the memories come flooding back! Especially, Glen's winning goal against Fulham (Champions!), and his performance against Preston, when Ian Moore finished off a run and centre by Glen, starting in his own half. Glen finished the scoring that day with a ground shot from the edge of the area. And then there was his point saving equaliser against high flying West Brom. In the end, it wasn't so much the end of season performances that let them down, when the team only lost one in the last eight games, as much as the run in February when the team lost three in a row against Crewe, Crystal Palace and Grimsby, all of whom finished in the bottom half of the table.

It was literally "ditto" the following season, as Burnley inspired by Messrs. Little and Payton ended up in seventh position once more. Of course, Glen got his usual goal against North End and, of course, Burnley suffered their almost annual humiliation by Manchester City, this time 1-5! (And Glen missed a penalty!) But at the close of the season, it wasn't the final 1-0 victory over Coventry that kept them down when the Clarets needed to score two, as much as the defensive record, which was one of the worst in the top half of the table!

Glen was one of those players who set the pulse racing, a player who could turn a game with one move. Because of this, there were those thousands (like myself!) who were excited before the game, just because he was playing. When he was out of the team, somehow the Burnley game was not quite the same. And in the end, we were all proved right. We could see the end was in sight and there didn't seem much that we, the fans, could do about it. Glen's contract was running out and the club couldn't match what he was surely worth. In a sentence, we couldn't afford Glen Little!

He went to Reading on loan, and that hurt because they were in the same division, and it looked as if they had promotion ambitions and we didn't! We were told that it was a move to save money! The following season, Glen went to Premiership Bolton on loan, but he never seemed to fit in at the Reebok. And so it was that at the end of 2003-04, Glen was transferred to Reading, still in the same league as the Clarets. It's nearly two years ago now, and I, for one Clarets fan, still miss the Cockney guy!

He came back to Turf Moor the other week with Reading; he was injured and I hoped he wouldn't play. Not just because I feared he would make mincemeat of our defence, but just because I didn't want to see him in a Reading jersey. I felt the same about seeing Jimmy Mac wearing a Stoke jersey, Willie Morgan in a United shirt, or Ralph Coates in a Spurs kit. It's the lot of we Burnley fans that we have had to bear for over a century. Since Crabtree went to Villa and Bruton went to Rovers; since Coates went to Spurs and Dobbo went to Everton, etc, etc. Does any other club suffer to the same extent? I sincerely doubt it. The players seem to benefit, the football club seems to be happy about it, it's just the fans who are left with their broken dreams.

Glen came on as sub, made a goal and was substituted himself. Some "fans" booed, far more applauded him, I just sat there and felt sort of empty. Still, as the old saying says: "Better to have loved and lost, than never to have loved at all!" Thanks Glen! But you'll always be a Claret!

Andy LOCHHEAD

1958-68

Centre forward
225 league games
105 goals

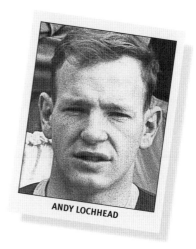

ANDY LOCHHEAD

Here at Burnley, we have had some very fine centre forwards since the War. But for me, three stand out from the rest – Pointer,

Lochhead and Payton. All quite different players, with their own gifts. And each will have their own supporters for the title, "the best" Take Andy Lochhead for instance.

Andy, a Scot from Renfrewshire came to Burnley in 1958, and he made his debut as a 19 year old against Manchester City in August 1960. It must have been an awesome occasion for the young Scot, standing in for International Ray Pointer and playing for the 1960 League Champions! The team that day read: Blacklaw; Angus, Elder; Adamson, Cummings, Miller; Meredith, McIlroy, Lochhead, Robson, Pilkington. And for the second time within seven days, Manchester City beat the Clarets, this time 3-1 at home!

His next game for the first team was at the controversial League Cup game away to Brentford when a "Burnley Reserve" team drew 1-1. (The "Reserve" team was fielded because of a glut of Division One, FA Cup, League Cup and European Cup fixtures that season. Altogether, the Clarets played in 61 games that season!) Andy's next game was equally as infamous too, as he played a major part in the next "Burnley Reserve" team, playing as the first team, this time in the Division One fixture against Chelsea. The reason this time for the "Reserves", was the number of injuries sustained during the previous week. A lot has been said about that game, but as a regular watcher of the Reserves that season, though mildly surprised, I had every confidence in the young team that played that memorable afternoon at Turf Moor. The Burnley team read: Furnell; Smith, Marshall; Walker, Cummings, Scott; Meredith, Lawson, Lochhead, Fenton and Harris. In a truly amazing game, "Burnley Reserves" drew 4-4 with Chelsea, with Andy Lochhead scoring twice. It was only a very late goal scored for Chelsea by the inimitable Jimmy Greaves which gained a point for Chelsea. Burnley were later fined £1,000 for fielding a weak team!

Along with several thousand others, I watched the development of the young Lochhead, and we saw some great performances from him as the Reserve team powered their way to the Central League title and the Lancashire Senior Cup win. However, it was not until early in the 1962-63 season, that Andy came into the first team as a regular. And to show the impression he created, regular centre forward, Ray Pointer moved over to inside right to accommodate the young Scot. The new look forward line was Connelly, Pointer, Lochhead, McIlroy, and Harris.

By this time, Andy was playing in the Scotland Under 23's team, and his goals for the Clarets became regular features. He was probably the tallest centre forward we had seen at Turf Moor for thirty years and together with his height, he brought his well built frame. He packed a terrific shot and he was lethal with his head. And he had immense skill with the ball on the ground.

In his first full season, Andy topped the scorers at Turf Moor with 20 goals These included eight goals in a six game sequence during September and October and two goals each against Blackburn, Sheffield United and Fulham. The following season, 63-64, he was top scorer again, with no doubt as to what was the highlight. Four goals in the 6-1 trouncing of Manchester United at Turf Moor on Boxing Day! Two days later, Andy scored again, this time at Old Trafford, but the Clarets went down 5-1 on that occasion. (Enter one George Best!). But not many players before or since have scored five against Manchester United in one season! (or in three days!) He also scored the seventh in the 7-2 thrashing of the famed Spurs in the last match of the season. What days those were to live in!

Andy Lochhead, by now one of the most feared centre forwards in the land, scored another 24 goals in 1964-65. By this time, he had moved over to inside right to partner Willie Irvine, and together they were a dynamic duo – 49 goals in 47 games. Included were Andy's two against Sheffield Wednesday and his hat-trick against Blackpool. But once again, Burnley reserved their highest score for their final game at Turf Moor against Chelsea. Andy Lochhead scored five in the Claret's 6-2 win, and in so doing, he joined Louis Page, Joe Anderson and Jimmy Robson as the only Burnley players to score five or more in a League match.

He did it again the following season, when he scored another five against Bournemouth in the FA Cup. This nap hand was accompanied by two goals each against Newcastle, Aston Villa and Leicester. And for the third time in four seasons, he topped the twenty goal mark. For the third time within five seasons, Andy Lochhead was the club's top scorer in 1966-67. That season he scored two against Tottenham, Chelsea, Southampton and West Brom, but his best day that season was when he scored all four in the 4-2 victory over Aston Villa. Another mini record that Andy Lochhead established on his goal scoring path was that he made himself Burnley's top scorer in European competitions with goals against Stuttgart (one), Lausanne (four), and Naples (one) in the European Fairs Cup.

In 1967-68, Burnley were beginning to slide from their Division One peaks. (For four consecutive seasons, they finished in 14th position) The goals weren't coming quite so easily. Whereas they had scored a century of goals for two seasons before, now they were glad to record fifty in a season. Whereas, Andy had recorded 21 League goals in 1964-65 and only finished second highest scorer at Turf Moor, in 1967-68, Frank Casper topped the list with just 14!

In October 1968, Andy Lochhead left Turf Moor for Leicester. In his nine years at Burnley, he had scored 128 goals in 265 games. He was the last of only six players in the club's history to complete a century of league goals. He stands alongside George Beel, Ray Pointer, Jimmy McIlroy, Louis Page and Bert Freeman as one of the great goal scoring personalities of the past 125 years. Everyone of us has his or her favourite players. Andy Lochhead remains one of mine, and I think that many thousands of Burnley fans who saw Andy Lochhead will agree with me.

Andy McCLUGGAGE

1924-31

Full back
213 league games
24 goals

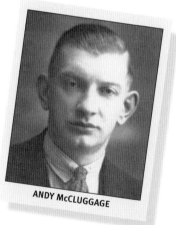

ANDY McCLUGGAGE

Andy McCluggage was one of Burnley's numerous Irish players over the years. And one of the best. He arrived at Turf Moor, via Bradford where he had established himself as first team full back, playing both right and left. He was also an Irish international by the time he came to Burnley.

Burnley were in desperate need of full backs in 1924 because the vintage days of Len Smelt and Dave Taylor were now past; and within a year, they found two – George Waterfield and Andy McCluggage They were to become one of the finest full back pairings ever at Burnley, or anywhere else for that matter. When Andy McCluggage played his first game for Burnley against Aston Villa in August 1925, it was a historic day. The team read: Dawson; McCluggage and Waterfield; Basnett, Hill and Parkin; Kelly, Freeman, Roberts, Beel and Page. That team included five English internationals – Dawson, Waterfield, Hill, Kelly, and Page, and an Irish international – Andy. Among the players were Burnley's all time top scorer, George Beel, and England's captain, Jack Hill. And the historic reason? The Clarets were beaten 10-0, still the club's record league defeat.

It was the first day of the new offside law, and Burnley just couldn't cope. Capewell scored for Villa in the first half minute and he went on to get a hat-trick before half time. Jack Hill was off the field injured for the best part of the game, and one Villa player said after the match: "It could have been 20!" And that was Andy's first game for the Clarets!

Despite the score, he was an instant success, and it was a pity that Burnley had to refuse to release him to play for Ireland against England, because of a crucial league game on the same day. That first season with Burnley, 1925-26 saw Andy McCluggage play in 35 games, scoring five goals, all from the penalty spot .Right from the word "Go!", McCluggage and Waterfield were the complete pairing. Curiously, George had been a left winger prior to his conversion at full back.

For the next few seasons, the only games that Andy McCluggage missed were either through injury or when he was playing for his native Ireland. He was a big, well built man, and a difficult player to get past. Occasionally, he doubled as left back when his pal George was absent, and curiously (for a change?), the pair switched positions for one game in 1930, when they appeared as Waterfield and McCluggage!

By the time, Andy McCluggage left Burnley in 1931, he had made 213 first team appearances, (172 of them partnering George Waterfield) and he had scored 24 goals mainly from the penalty spot. That is surely a record number of goals from any Burnley full back, and he even scored another for Ireland during his eleven international appearances. In their heyday, the names of McCluggage and Waterfield were as famous locally and nationally as Halley, Boyle 'n' Watson. My dad thought the world of big Andy, and I can't say more than that!

Colin
McDONALD

1953-59

Goalkeeper
186 league games

COLIN McDONALD

What if? What if Colin McDonald hadn't broken his leg in Dublin that day in March 1959? What would he have achieved? What might Burnley have achieved? What would have happened to Adam Blacklaw? We could go on – what would have happened to the international careers of other goalkeepers like Eddie Hopkinson, Ron Springett, Alan Hodgkinson – and yes, even Gordon Banks. Let me explore the possibilities. McDonald would have been 36 by the time the 1966 World Cup took place.. Too old? Gordon Banks was still playing for England when he was 35 and would surely have gone on but for injury. Ray Clemence was 34 and still an England international. Peter Shilton was 41 and still England's number one. Are you getting my drift? As one who saw Colin McDonald perform regularly, I have often wondered on those lines. And surely, all those Clarets fans who appreciated his greatness week by week, have done the same? And most of all, Colin himself must often have wondered?

But maybe we are racing on too fast for our younger Clarets? Let's fill in the background. Colin McDonald came to Turf Moor as a 17 year old goalkeeper in 1948. Due to the longevity of Jimmy Strong and the faithful work of his successor, Des Thompson, it was 1954 before Colin McDonald made his somewhat inauspicious debut, in the 5-1 away defeat at Aston Villa. The Burnley team in that memorable game of the 1953-54 season read; McDonald; Aird, Winton; Adamson, Binns, Seith; Gray, McIlroy, Holden, Shannon, Pilkington. (Incidentally, the Clarets were on a bad run at the time. They only won one of their last seven games, and still finished seventh in the league at the end!)

But Colin kept his place for the last five games of the season, and indeed for the next five seasons too. McDonald was above all reliable. Never spectacular, rarely risky. Always dependable, and more than capable, he was "always there". It was probably his sense of anticipation and his positional skills which made Colin make his job look so easy. Which of course, it wasn't! Those were different days as far as football was concerned. Teams sought to attack and the Clarets were no different. "Clean sheets" were rare, but Burnley's defence could still match any in the land. In 1954-55, the Clarets had the best defence in Division One, the second best in 1955-56, and the best once again in 1956-57. And surely, the presence of Colin "Mac" in goals had something to do with that? And whilst we're into statistics, the Burnley team with McDonald in goal never finished below tenth position in Division One!

We should admit it that during the 1950's, we were spoilt at Turf Moor; we took excellence as a matter of fact. We watched some of Britain's finest players every week, and often felt it was our duty to criticise them if necessary. Jimmy Adamson, Jimmy McIlroy, Colin McDonald all had their critics, however, little they deserved them! Some folk are never happy! But McDonald just seemed to excel week after week. And at last the nation began to sit up and notice.

In March 1958, he was selected for the Football League, and two months later he won his first England cap when he played for England in the 1-1 draw in Moscow. .During those days, England had a bit of a problem with finding a regular goalkeeper. There had been eight within four years, 1954-58 – Gil Merrick, Ray Wood, Bert Williams, Ron Baynham, Reg Matthews, Ted Ditchburn, Alan Hodgkinson and Eddie Hopkinson. But when McDonald came on the scene, how things changed! Within a couple of games, he had made the position his own.

He went to Sweden as a major part of the England team in the 1958 World Cup, and he played in all four of England's games. He played in the first three group matches against Russia (again!), Brazil, and Austria, which all resulted in draws, 2-2, 0-0 and 2-2. In the next round, England were beaten by Russia (again!) 1-0, and so the England team came home. But during his time in Sweden, Colin had caught the world's eye, especially after a superlative display against World Champions, Brazil. His fine performances were recognised ,when he was voted the outstanding goalkeeper in the 1958 World Cup tournament. The world was at his feet!

The following season, 1958-59, Colin was back at his brilliant best with his Burnley colleagues, and also alongside his England team-mates. All seemed well. The Clarets were as usual(!) in the top half of the table, and England were unbeaten since the World Cup with a 5-0 revenge win against Russia (again!) and draws 3-3 and 2-2 against Northern Ireland and Wales. That is, until 17 March 1958. I was at Turf Moor that night with my dad. The Clarets were at home on a Tuesday night against Blackpool, and Colin McDonald was absent, because he was playing for the Football League against the League of Ireland, in Dublin. It was announced over the tannoy at half-time, to a stunned Turf Moor, that Colin "Mac" had been carried off, with a broken leg. Things looked bad.

But matters were even worse, as it turned out. Complications set in and Colin contracted pneumonia, which for a time was life threatening. Fortunately, after some time, he recovered his health, but we were never to see him play at Burnley for the first team again. In 1961, he sadly accepted that his playing career at Burnley was over and he left the club. It was the worst moment of his career, and one of the saddest times in my memories of this club of ours.

Which brings us back to our opening question, "What if?" What if Colin McDonald's life hadn't been turned upside down by that tragic injury? I imagine that "Mac" could have gained a hundred International caps. (No joking – he wouldn't have even been 40 by that time, and Peter Shilton went on till he was 41!) And as for the Clarets, it could have been a different tale altogether. (And this is with no disrespect to Adam Blacklaw, a vital cog in the Championship machinery) A lot of questions remain unanswered forever since March 1959.

Looking back now, I've seen some good goalkeepers in my time – Bert Williams, Ted Ditchburn and Adam Blacklaw come to mind. One or two who were truly great – Frank Swift, Bert Trautmann and Gordon Banks were among them. But I would rate Colin McDonald to be the best of them all, and because he was still in his 20s, maybe we never saw the best from him. What if …?

Jimmy McILROY

1950-63

Inside forward
439 league games
116 goals

JIMMY McILROY

When I was a lad, it seemed as if every team had a class inside forward – someone who could control the ball, and the game, someone who was the brains behind the team. He was an entertainer and the crowds would roll up, simply to see this player who could work wonders with the ball and inspire his team. Len Shackleton, Raich Carter, Peter Doherty, Ivor Broadis, Wilf Mannion – my dad took me all over to see these players. Such players gave you a thrill just to see them run out before the game and shoot in prior to the kick off!

Little did we realise in 1950, that here at Burnley we were about to see one of the best every week at Turf Moor. Because, of course, it was Burnley we supported – this small Lancashire cotton town of cobbled streets and gas lamps. Youngsters like me had been fed a diet of memories by our dads and grandads of the artistry of Bob Kelly, 25 years earlier. It all seemed like a dream that our parents had had. Did Bob Kelly ever exist?

Jimmy McIlroy was signed by Burnley manager Frank Hill in 1950, as an 18 year old from Glentoran for £8,000. He made his debut the following week at Turf Moor in front of 8,646 people in the Central League game against Chesterfield Reserves. The date was 25 March 1950, and though the young Irishman played a superb game, it is doubtful if many people there realised how great a player he was to become. The following October (1950), regular forward Harry Potts left the club for Everton, and the week after his departure, young Jimmy made his League debut, away to Sunderland. The team that day read: Strong; Woodruff, Mather; Attwell, Cummings, Bray; Stephenson, Morris, Holden, McIlroy and Hays. Personally, it was the following Saturday, 28 October 1950, that I first saw "Jimmy Mac". That is a guaranteed date, as my dad and I never missed a home game for year after year. (Having lived in Newtownards during the war, I felt from the start a kinship with this Ulster exile. Until then, the only non-English player I had seen in a Burnley jersey was Welshman Billy Morris!)

From that first game at Sunderland, Jimmy retained his position at inside left. It wasn't until his third season at Turf Moor that he was moved permanently to the inside right spot, in place of Billy Morris. (Truth to say, he was equally at home in either position, being completely two footed, and he often played on the left for his native Ireland.) Less than a year after his Turf Moor debut, Jimmy was chosen for the Irish international team to play Scotland, partnering his ex-Glentoran colleague, Billy Bingham on the right wing.

The Burnley team in the early fifties was undergoing rapid change from the "iron curtain" defensive team of 1947, to a side adopting a far more attacking approach with fast young wingers like Roy Stephenson and Brian Pilkington, and skilled ball players like Jimmy McIlroy and Les Shannon. There were some fine performances, and goals came far more regularly than for many seasons. (During one six match unbeaten sequence in 1952, the team scored 20 goals – unheard of!)

Early in 1952-53, after a run of eight unbeaten games, the Clarets found themselves at the top of Division One, (the first time for over 30 years!) A strong rumour that Spurs had offered £50,000 for McIlroy and Elliott was denied at Turf Moor. By this time, Jimmy was beginning to score a few goals as well as helping to create them for Bill Holden and Les Shannon. He scored twice against both Stoke City and Manchester United. (Both games were won 3-1 and both games were away from home!) Indeed that season of 1952-53 saw "Jimmy Mac" finish third top scorer with 12 goals, behind Holden and Shannon.

How the memories come flooding back now as an old man remembers a young boy beginning to idolise a young Irishman.

1953-54 was the season when we beat Manchester United, three times, including the never to be forgotten Third Round Cup Tie. That was the game that was 2-2 after only six minutes! With the score 3-3, Jimmy Mac got the fourth before the Clarets ran out 5-3 winners. (That afternoon, I was on the Longside, uncovered of course, in the midst of the 52,847 crowd. My friend, Pete and I started the game stood on a pile of bricks at the back, before squirming our way down to the front by half time!).

The mid-50s saw the emergence (in my eyes) of the scheming, tactical genius of McIlroy. We in the crowd there, were to witness the new style of football strategy that Burnley became famous for, as they introduced short corners and double free kicks. (My dad used to joke about whether it would be plan 12 or plan 15 that Messrs McIlroy and Adamson would try from a dead ball situation.) Soon, teams across the land copied Burnley's tactics. By now, Jimmy McIlroy had become known throughout the country as the cultured ball player that we in Burnley and Belfast knew him to be.

1956 wasn't such a great year for Jimmy, as due to an ankle ligament injury in the 4-4 draw at Roker Park, he missed the next dozen games. (It did provide me with an extra bonus, as I won a national competition in *"Soccer Star"* when we had to write a letter to our favourite player. Guess who I wrote to?) I wasn't so unusual – every young Burnley schoolboy idolised the man, and we would spend our Saturday evenings reliving every move he had made that afternoon! Once at Turf Moor, whilst I was waiting for Jimmy to emerge after the game, right winger Doug Newlands came out first, and I sent him back to the dressing room with a request for the great man's autograph! But it wasn't just the schoolboys who were following "Mac", he was making the nation sit up and pay attention to his skills. Such as when in 1956, he was chosen to represent Great Britain in a game against the Rest of Europe, or when he scored the equaliser for Ireland in the 1-1 draw against England in 1956.

Stanley Matthews said of him in the 1950's: "Had he been born an Englishman, I feel his name would have been one of the biggest in world football." Peter Doherty, one of the "greats" himself and Irish team manager said of Jimmy: "He is a World wonder inside forward." Tom Finney said: "Jimmy might be called Britain's greatest inside forward." Whilst Matt Busby said: "Jimmy possesses something which is only shared by the all-time greats." Jimmy Greaves has written: "McIlroy, stocky and almost arrogant, inspired everyone around him with wonderfully imaginative and intelligent positioning and passing."

In 1956-57 and the following season too, Jimmy did something he had never done before – he topped the Burnley goalscorers – 16 goals in the first season and 19 goals, the year after. He scored twice against Arsenal, Sheffield Wednesday, Cardiff, Spurs, Leicester and Bolton, and he notched up hat-tricks against Leicester and in the memorable 9-0 FA Cup Tie against New Brighton. (There has always been a self effacing modesty about the man too. When Burnley in later years beat Penrith, 9-0, Jimmy, then a reporter, rang me up to ask if Burnley had ever scored nine in a Cup Tie before. And it gave me quite a thrill as a historian to say: "Yes in 1957 against New Brighton. And you played and you scored a hat-trick!" The great man had forgotten!)

Just as a taste of what it was like to watch "Jimmy Mac" in the 1950s, listen to this report of the Manchester City v Burnley game in 1958: "McIlroy illuminated the murk of Manchester with one of his star performances. He was the mentor, the master magician whose sorcery conjured the ball round, through, between heavier bodies and left them sprawling. They tackled him in pairs, they crowded him in threes; he showed them the ball, flicked it away from them, worked it on with little skips and feints and shuffles, while the crowd gazed on in silent wonder. He was so baffling that one received the impression that had the Laws of Football allowed it, he would have waved one of his magic feet over the ball three times, and produced it reduced in size from the referee's pocket! Once, Hannah, no mean artiste as a ball player, chased McIlroy almost to a corner flag as if trying to find out just how he achieved this uncanny mastery." This sort of thing was going on week after week, and we at Burnley took it all for granted – we had come to totally accept the genius in our midst. Listen again to another report, this time from the Arsenal v Burnley game in 1959: "The injured McIlroy did enough on one leg to make observers wonder to what depths of humiliation Arsenal would have sank, if he had been able to bewilder them on two!"

Time and space forbids us to elaborate on what happened in 1959-60 – it is football history. Players like Pointer, Robson and Connelly revelled in the service given to them by McIlroy, and between them they scored 69 goals that season. Everyone present

Jimmy McIlroy, 1950-63

"Had he been born an Englishman, I feel his name would have been one of the biggest in world football" – Stanley Matthews. "Jimmy might be called Britain's greatest inside forward" – Tom Finney. Can there be a greater accolade?

has their own memories of that momentous season. I can instantly recall the cup tie (2-2) at Bradford City, (was I the only person there to notice that the band struck up"Mack the Knife"as he came out on the pitch?), the vast crowd that night, the following week at the replay, the vital point won at Blackpool the week after Easter, the penalties which Jimmy McIlroy "ghosted" past various goalkeepers, and the last match at Manchester City. With the final minutes ticking away, Brian Pilkington lying just off the pitch injured, and Jimmy McIlroy it seemed defying the entire City team by holding onto the ball at the corner flag, and the referee looking at his watch, the tension was unbearable. BUT WE WON! WE WON!!!!!

In 1960-61 we had the European Cup games, with Jimmy scoring in the home game against Reims and hitting the post in the final minute of the 4-1 defeat in Hamburg. In the League, though the Clarets finished fourth, at times their football was too staggering to believe. Twenty goals in four games in October (six against Chelsea, away, five each against Fulham and United, and four against Rovers, away.) was followed by 22 in five games (five each against Wolves, Bolton away and Arsenal away, four against Spurs away, and three against Leicester) On 16 occasion, the Clarets scored four or more goals in a game! And Jimmy McIlroy was the secret of their success. But hardly a secret – the entire country knew of him!

The following season, 1961-62 was even more successful, and though the Clarets just missed out on both League and Cup, on 11 occasion they scored four goals or more. Most memorable were the 17 goals they scored in three successive away games (two sixes and a five!). These were wonderful days to be a Burnley supporter, and "Jimmy Mac" was making football reporters search for new superlatives after a sequence of magnificent performances. Unfortunately, he was injured with 10 games to play, and Burnley failed to win any of the five games in which he was absent. (Just a couple of victories in those games would have given Burnley the title!) At the end of the season, Jimmy Adamson was chosen as Footballer of the Year, whilst"Mac"was runner up!

Jimmy McIlroy began his 13th season at Turf Moor in August 1962. None of us could foresee what was to happen. It was a good season as the Clarets went on an unbeaten sequence of 10 games from September until November (one victory was a 5-2 away win against Manchester United, when McIlroy scored for the third game running). One of the season's best performances was at the end of the year, when the Clarets beat Sheffield Wednesday 4-0. The newspaper said: "Despite the ice rink surface, this was a vintage McIlroy who gave a performance his fans won't forget for a long time, highlighted by that magnificent burst, four minutes from time, which led to Pointer scoring the final goal. Who said McIlroy is finished?" This was followed by a remarkable 3-0 Cup victory at Tottenham, and a long spell of no games due to the extreme weather conditions that winter.

In March, Burnley lost in a Cup replay at Anfield in the last minute, but it was nothing compared to the shock that hit the town the next day, when "Jimmy Mac" was placed on the transfer list. "I couldn't believe it" said "Mac". Letters of protest poured into the local paper, petitions were begun, expressions of protest were daubed on walls in the town, as supporters objected to the transfer of their idol of over a decade. The club gave their reason for the action. They said that they felt Jimmy McIlroy was not maintaining the consistency of ability which he was able to command. It was said that he was not giving the club the wholehearted effort which was expected of him.

His fans disagreed. And that day the club and thousands of supporters agreed to differ and went their separate ways. Gates at Turf Moor, which had reached 44,000 in November crashed to 14,000 in May. The following season, they dropped to 10,000, and the year after, to less than 10,000, for the first time since the war. Many people never went back to Turf Moor ever again. My Uncle Jim was just one. My dad, after a lifetime of support, certainly lost a lot of interest, as did we all

Jimmy soon went to Stoke for £25,000, a mere pittance of his true value. My father summed up many local feelings when he said that the club should have built him a house at Gawthorpe so that he could have passed on some of his expertise! I went to watch him a few times when he played for Stoke. But it was not the same, nor was Turf Moor for many seasons afterwards. I think that everyone felt the same. Some players over the years have made going to a football match an exciting occasion. You looked forward to seeing them. Even if it was a poor game, even if the Clarets were losing, the sheer pleasure of watching a particular player made your heart beat faster. Jimmy McIlroy was such a player. In later years, I felt similar feelings for other players – Ray Pointer, Ralph Coates, Martin Dobson. But I had never known it before "Jimmy Mac" Matt Busby once said of "Jimmy Mac":"Only those who follow Burnley regularly could calculate his great value." I still well remember the last time that we saw Jimmy play on Turf Moor in a claret jersey. It was the night of John Angus's testimonial, when a team of "Vintage Clarets" played the Youth team. A Lancashire lady sat in front of my dad and I, burst into tears when he came on the pitch, as she said to her wide eyed little boy, "That's Jimmy McIlroy, son. that's Jimmy McIlroy!" And there were tears in more eyes than hers that night. (And he scored!)

In later years, the Football League included Jimmy McIlroy as one of the greatest 100 players to have ever played. We in Burnley have even petitioned for him to be knighted! A legend in our own lifetime.

Willie MORGAN

1962-68, 1975-76

Winger
195 league games
19 goals

WILLIE MORGAN

Willie Morgan! Even now the name excites me! We were indeed privileged in the 1960's to see players of the ilk of McIlroy and Adamson in the first team, but it was equally exciting to watch the Reserves every fortnight. Crowds in excess of 10,000 came every week to see the up and coming talent on show – the latest products of the youth system at Turf Moor. And what talent there was to see! Players in Burnley Reserves seemed every bit as good (and many would say"Better!") as the excellent players we had in the first team. As if to prove the point, when Manchester United bought John Connelly in 1964, a member of the United board said to me in some sort of consolation: "You've got an even better player to take his position – Willie Morgan!" Even then, United knew of the man's existence! The two Willies – Morgan and Irvine were a sheer joy to watch as they blossomed in the Reserves – true international players in the making. Willie Morgan was a right winger of the classic mould – tricky dribbling which made the opposing defender's life a nightmare, followed by pin point centres. The Turf Moor crowd loved him. After having had players on the right wing like Billy Gray, Doug Newlands and John Connelly, we could recognise a class winger when we saw one. And Willie Morgan was such a player.

He made his first team debut as a 19 year old towards the end of the 1962-63 season, in the away game against Sheffield Wednesday, when the Burnley team read: Blacklaw; Angus, Elder; Walker, Talbut, Miller; Morgan, Robson, Lochhead, Bellamy and Connelly. With Cummings amd McIlroy both having left that season, it was a time of change. And players like Willie Morgan heralded a bright future for the Clarets!

For much of the following season, here at Turf Moor, we had the sheer luxury of Willie Morgan on the right wing and John Connelly on the left – few clubs have been able to boast of such a pair of wingers in the same team. So good they were, that United bought them both!! A typical team towards the end of the 1963-64 season would read: Blacklaw; Angus, Elder; O'Neill, Talbut, Miller; Morgan, Irvine, Lochhead, Bellamy, and Connelly. Wow! This was the sort of team that beat Manchester United 6-1 at Turf Moor on Boxing Day and Tottenham, 7-2 on the last day of the season. Incidentally, Willie scored his first two goals for the Clarets in the Boxing Day massacre, and two days later Matt Busby introduced George Best into the United attack (winning 5-1 at Old Trafford!) In later seasons, Best and Morgan would pair up as United's wingers.

Willie Morgan on his day at Turf Moor was unstoppable; it seemed that he could bewilder even the best of British full backs, and from his centres, Messrs.Irvine and Lochhead made hay whilst the sun shone. From 1964 to 1968, Irvine and Lochhead scored well over a century of goals between them – 167 to be exact! And if we give credit where credit's due, then the vast majority of those goals stemmed from young Morgan on the right wing.

For a while, the Clarets threatened to have a renaissance in the mid-60s of their triumphs five years earlier, but the best that the club achieved was third place in the league in 1965-66. But we flattered to deceive and that was our best league placing for the next 40 plus seasons. Of course, it couldn't last, and Willie Morgan became yet another statistic in the "Players Sold" column of the Burnley balance sheet. Just before the start of the 1968-69 season, Willie asked for a transfer and quite an auction began. Leeds began with an opening bid of £75,000, but eventually our hero followed John Connelly to Old Trafford for £117,000. And with Willie Morgan having left (following Blacklaw, Elder, Harris and Irvine), was it any wonder that the attendances at the first two games that season only totalled 26,000. This at Turf Moor where not so long before, the club had commanded gates of 30,000, 40,000 and even occasionally, 50,000. The writing was on the wall!

But for those of us who were there to see it all, the days of Willie Morgan & Co at Turf Moor in the mid-60s bring back glorious memories. The name might still excite, but the memories send a shiver up your spine. We haven't seen his like since.

Eddie MOSSCROP

1912-22

Winger
176 league games
19 goals

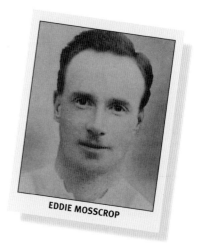

EDDIE MOSSCROP

A native of Southport, Eddie Mosscrop came to Burnley in the summer of 1912. His debut for the first team was on 7 September 1912 on the opening day of the 1912-13 season. Having just failed in their promotion bid the previous season the Turf Moor team were on the verge of greatness. The next six seasons would see them reach the heights of football fame.

The Burnley team that played Glossop on that September day read: Dawson; Reid, Taylor; Bradshaw, Boyle and Watson; Mosscrop, Lindley, Freeman, Picken and Mountford. The game was won 2-1.

Curiously, for those who know their Clarets history, Eddie Mosscrop, later to become an established and international left winger in the game, began his days at Turf Moor on the right wing. Indeed, in his first two seasons at Burnley, Eddie played far more games on the right than on the left. But as I've tried to explain elsewhere, players were completely two footed in those days!

Eddie was fast and very tricky – a handful to mark and a delight to watch. He was always one of my grandad's favourite players, and though I was born half a century after Eddie Mosscrop, I grew up admiring the man – thanks to grandad! Interest in the team was very high in 1912-13, as shown by the fact that 8,000 paid 2d each to see the public practice match. Besides playing football, Eddie was first and foremost a schoolteacher (life in football was somewhat different in 1912). Because of this, Eddie was unable to play in midweek games or in games involving long weekend journeys, owing to his teaching commitments.

That 1912-13 season was a great time for the Burnley team, as they finished runners up in Division Two and reached the Semi Final of the FA Cup for the very first time. Eddie was a member of the team that won 11 consecutive games, as well as the team that beat Blackburn Rovers at Ewood, 1-0 in the Quarter Finals, and drew 0-0 with Sunderland in the Semi Final. Though Bert Freeman captured the headlines with his 36 goals that season, many of them came from the twinkling feet of Eddie Mosscrop on the right wing. Incidentally, for their successes, the Burnley players shared between them £220 for being runners up in Division Two and £165 for reaching the Semi Final!

The following season was to see both Burnley and Eddie reach the heights. The club established themselves back in Division One, but their great story was being written in the FA Cup. Beating South Shields and Derby County (including the 40 year old Steve Bloomer) in the first rounds, Burnley found themselves drawn at home against local rivals Bolton Wanderers. Prices were raised for the game to 1s for the ground and 3s for the stand and 32,734 came to Turf Moor on a fine February afternoon Many people walked from Bolton, arriving long before 10am, and nine excursion trains made the trip from Bolton to Burnley. Burnley won the game 3-0 and were drawn away to League Champions, Sunderland, the same team which had beaten Burnley in the Semi Final 12 months previously.

Burnley, c1920

The period from 1912 to 1922 was the most successful decade in the club's history, winning promotion, becoming League Champions and winning the FA Cup.

A record crowd for Sunderland of 34,581 were at Roker Park that day to see Burnley come away with a 0-0 draw against the Sunderland team of internationals – Ness, Cuggy, Mordue, Buchan & Co! History was made again at Turf Moor the following week, when a crowd over 10,000 greater than any previous attendance jammed into the ground to see the replayed Cup Tie. Altogether, 49,734 people filled Turf Moor and they paid a record £2,838. "In the history of Burnley Football Club, it will be recorded that one of the most brilliant achievements was the victory over Sunderland, which paved the way to the Semi Final for the second season in succession." So wrote one newspaper in retrospect. The Wearsiders were routed; Hodgson scored within four minutes, and then Lindley got a second. Connor scored a late goal for Sunderland but the result was never in doubt. The *"Daily News"* said; "It was a great triumph for Burnley – one of the best in the club's history, looked at from whatever point of view one likes. They were a great side, fore and aft. There was nothing better in the match than the wing play of new international Mosscrop – easily the best forward on view." Soon after the game, Eddie Mosscrop was chosen to play for the English League against the Scottish League, played on Turf Moor, 21 March 1914.

It was Eddie Mosscrop who made the goal which won the Semi

Final against Sheffield United: "Nesbitt centred brilliantly right to the feet of Mosscrop. Mosscrop trapped the ball and touched it back to Boyle, who espying an opening amid the players, shot the ball into the net with terrific force." It was the winning goal and Burnley were through to their first ever FA Cup Final at Crystal Palace.

Of course, the rest is history, of how Burnley and Liverpool played in the first ever royally attended FA Cup Final, Bert Freeman's winning goal, and Burnley's triumphal return to the town, complete with the Cup! And Eddie Mosscrop, now a regular left winger was an indispensable part of that great team – Sewell (Dawson); Bamford, Taylor; Halley, Boyle and Watson; Nesbitt, Lindley, Freeman, Hodgson and Mosscrop. Within a few months, the Great War had begun (Eddie Mosscrop served in Salonika). I always like to think that as the soldiers left this land for overseas, many of them took memories not only of families, but of the Burnley team who were national figures at the time.

Just to catch a flavour of Mosscrop at his most magical, read this report of the Burnley v Bolton game: "Mosscrop began cautiously, almost timorously, when he found that both Gimblett and Nuttall did not hesitate to use their weight. Neither of them will forget very readily what he did when he got the measure of them. He skipped, he pranced, he cut in, darted out, he twisted and pivoted, and all the time, he did what he liked with the ball."

After the War, by which time, Eddie Mosscrop was an established English International player, the Burnley team gradually recouped, and 1919-20 saw them finish runners up for the first time in their history. (One only wonders what that side of Halley, Boyle'n Watson & Co. would have achieved in football, but for the war?) Eddie played on, but was injured badly in the first game of the 1920-21 season in the home game against Bradford City. Reserve left winger, Walt Weaver took his place, and established himself on the left wing until Eddie returned in the New Year. He continued to bewilder opposing defences, until one day he wasn't quite fast enough. On 20 March 1920, the Sunderland defender Coverdale, kicked Mosscrop up, and "Mossy" (to quote the newspaper of the day) "went spinning like a catherine wheel".

The end of Eddie Mosscrop's playing career can be said to have dawned on that day, because sciatica set in, from which he suffered for the rest of his life. Eddie played on bravely despite great pain, until November 1922 when he had to call it a day, still aged only 30. The great Eddie Mosscrop achieved everything there was to win in football – League Championship, FA Cup Winner and English International caps. He was truly one of Turf Moor's legends. Just as my grandad repeatedly told me!

Billy NESBITT

1911-23

Winger
172 league games
19 goals

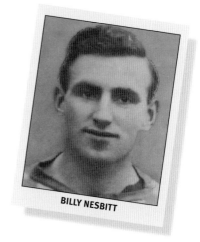

BILLY NESBITT

Curiously following on from Eddie Mosscrop comes Billy Nesbitt. Their stories were quite parallel for many years, and they were great colleagues and team mates. Rivals too for a time.

Billy was a local man from Portsmouth (near Todmorden) and he arrived at Turf Moor in September 1911. It was a period of rebuilding at Turf Moor – Bert Freeman had arrived earlier that year to join Jerry Dawson and Billy Watson in the first team. Teddy Hodgson arrived in the same month as Billy Nesbitt and the month after, Tommy Boyle came to the club from Barnsley. With such players in their ranks, the club's performances improved by leaps and bounds, and with their successes, the crowds rolled up in even greater numbers. Three times that season, the gates receipts record was shattered by hundreds of pounds and on 16 March 1912 came a highwater mark for the Turf Moor ground, the first gate over 30,000 when Derby County came to play at Burnley. At the time, Derby, complete with Steve Bloomer, were lying third in Division Two, whilst Burnley were on top of the Division. The result was 0-0. But we are racing ahead.

Billy Nesbitt had made his League debut just a month before the Derby game when Burnley entertained Barnsley at Turf Moor, winning 3-0. The Burnley team that day read: Dawson; Reid, Taylor; McLaren, Boyle, Watson; Nesbitt, Lindley, Freeman, Hodgson and Harris. Billy was a fast and clever right winger and his arrival in the first team coincided with a run of six consecutive victories and 10 games without defeat. The following season, 1912-13 was a difficult one for Billy as he faced competition for the right wing berth, first from Eddie Mosscrop and then from Jim Bellamy, "the crack inside right from Motherwell" whom the club had bought for £1,000.

Billy's disappointment at only filling a reserve spot continued into the 1913-14 season, and his few first team appearances were as left winger filling in for Will Husband or Tom Charlton. It was New Year's Day 1914 which saw the change as far as Billy Nesbitt was concerned. He came in at his best position of right winger, whilst the player who had held that position for the previous 12 months, Eddie Mosscrop reverted to his role as left winger. The change took effect immediately. Burnley went nine games into 1914 unbeaten, including a 6-2 win away at Sheffield Wednesday and a three game run in the FA Cup which took them to the Third Round against Bolton.

The game proved a great triumph for the Burnley team with Bert Freeman scoring after half an hour and Hodgson and Halley making it 3-0 in the second half. "MAGNIFICENT VICTORY" ran the newspaper headlines, as Burnley beat the team who were third in Division One at the time, and who included such stars as Vizard and Smith. The *"Burnley Gazette"* reported: "Dawson did his job to perfection; Bamford and Taylor were towers of strength; the half backs were superb, and Nesbitt had his best game of the season – all three goals coming from his wing. Exit Bolton!"

Burnley beat League Champions Sunderland in the next round, and history was created for the Turf Moor team as they beat Sheffield United in the Semi Final before beating Liverpool in the Final at Crystal Palace. The record books may show that Tommy Boyle scored the Semi Final winner and Bert Freeman scored the Cup Final winner. But newspaper reports of the day tell the true story. And that was that Billy Nesbitt helped to create both goals. In the Burnley v Sheffield United Semi Final replay at Everton, the score was 0-0, when with 17 minutes to go "Nesbitt, who had scarcely played upto his true form, centred brilliantly, right to the feet of Mosscrop. Mosscrop trapped the ball and touched it back to Boyle, who espying an opening amid the players, shot the ball into the net with terrific force." And so to Crystal Palace. The score was 0-0 at halftime and Bert Freeman's goal came 13 minutes after the interval: "From a throw in on the right, Nesbitt banged the ball across to Hodgson, who had to compete with Longworth. It was a great leap that Hodgson made before he reached the ball above the head of Longworth, but he managed to get his head to the ball, and directed it across to Freeman. Like a flash, the Burnley centre was on the ball, and he snapped up the opportunity without hesitation. Campbell in the Liverpool goal had no chance of saving, and Freeman was almost overwhelmed by the exuberance of the Burnley team who swarmed around him." (*"Burnley Gazette"*) OK, I know that quote has appeared elsewhere in this collection of biographies, but who's complaining?!

It was a fact that Tommy Boyle shouted at his team, but he shouted louder than ever at poor Billy Nesbitt who was stone deaf. It must have been a source of amusement to the crowd, and it certainly scared some of the Burnley players when Boyle started his rantings. But his deafness didn't seem to affect his play, and Billy Nesbitt continued to be a great success on the right wing. Probably due to his disability, Billy was available to play for Burnley during the War, and he clocked up many games during the conflict.

After the war, Billy Nesbitt struck up a famous partnership on the right wing with the up and coming Bob Kelly, and the pair became famous throughout the country. Because of his size, Billy Nesbitt, like his left wing colleague Eddie Mosscrop, was often the subject of heavy tackles and injury cost him many games in 1919-20. But he was there again the following season, and after missing the first two games through an injury from the previous season, Billy Nesbitt never missed another game throughout the Championship year of 20-21; indeed, other than Watson and Anderson, Billy played more games that famous season than any player.

If he had been a key source of centres for Bert Freeman, so too his supply of pin point centres was invaluable to Freeman's successor, "Joe Andy". A couple of quotes help remind us of the quality of Nesbitt's play. Against Oldham Athletic (a game which Burnley won 7-1), the *"Burnley News"* wrote: "The play of the Burnley side was too staggering for words. Kelly was surely an inspiration to see, co-operating with Nesbitt in a manner which brought the pair cheer after cheer. Theirs was surely the acme of scientific skill" And against

Sunderland in the final game of that memorable season, when the club received the League Championship trophy, the *"Burnley News"* reported: "Nesbitt and Kelly levelled the scores for Burnley after Sunderland had gone two ahead. Rarely have Kelly and Nesbitt operated better than on Saturday. Nesbitt had the Sunderland defence in a hopeless tangle, and seemed able to do just as he liked."

Altogether. Billy Nesbitt and Bob Kelly paired up on the right wing for Burnley well over a 100 times, forming one of the most famous wing partnerships in the country. Their Turf Moor story closed when Billy finally called it a day through injury at the end of the 1922-23 season. On his final game, away at Cardiff, the much changed Burnley team read: Moorwood; Smelt, Taylor; Watson, Bassnett, Morgan; Nesbitt, Lindsay, Kelly, Cross and Weaver. Billy Nesbitt remains as one of the best right wingers that the Clarets have had in the last 100 years, standing rightly with the likes of Bruton, Connelly and Morgan.

I last heard of Billy Nesbitt in the 1960's. My Uncle, another lifelong Clarets fan, lived in Blackpool, and he regularly saw Billy, now an elderly man, selling newspapers on the corner of Talbot Square. You couldn't have put Stanley Matthews, Tom Finney or even "Gazza" in the same role. Because none of them ever won both the League Championship and the FA Cup. Billy did!

Keith NEWTON

1972-78

Full back
209 league games
5 goals

KEITH NEWTON

These days, there seems to be among some younger Burnley fans a hatred and derision of all things connected with Blackburn Rovers. It was not always so – respect and very keen rivalry yes, but never hatred! In fact some of our best players have played for both teams – Jackie Bruton, John Connelly, Adam Blacklaw, and more recently, Keith Newton.

It would have seemed that when Keith Newton, aged 30, arrived at Turf Moor in the summer of 1972, his best playing days were over and his career was fading fast. He had played 10 years for Blackburn, three years with Everton (including a League Championship season in 1970) and had gained 27 England caps in the process. But the end was far from sight! For many of we Burnley fans, the best was yet to be.

The Clarets were back in Division Two, and it still seemed strange for us after 24 years in the top flight. Nevertheless, Jimmy Adamson, with his so called "Team of the 70's" was intent on regaining a place in the First Division, and after an average season in the Second Division, Jimmy signed Keith Newton. There was a problem in defence now that John Angus had retired, and in 1971-72, six players had played in the full back role – Angus, Wilson, Docherty, Cliff, Nulty and Thomson. To solve the problem, veteran Keith Newton was signed. Problem solved!

For the next five seasons, we at Turf Moor witnessed some of the finest full back performances we had ever seen. We saw it all – class, elegance, coolness, composure, skill, confidence – Keith Newton had it all. Couple all these qualities with immaculate ball control and vast experience, and here we had the supreme full back.

Keith's first game for Burnley was in the opening match at Turf Moor in August 1972, against Carlisle United. The team read: Stevenson; Docherty, Newton; Dobson, Waldron, Thomson; Ingham, Casper, Fletcher, Thomas and James. That team stayed the same all season. There were only three changes in the next 12 months with the introduction of Doug Collins and Geoff Nulty, and just for three games, Eddie Cliff. Keith Newton was one of six ever presents, which must be a club record of some kind.

From the start, the Docherty-Newton pairing gelled. It was the best full back partnership we had seen at Turf Moor since the days of Angus and Elder. Few players, if anyone at all in the history of the club, have begun their Turf Moor careers in such a successful manner as did Keith Newton. It was November (after 16 games) before the team lost their first League game, and it was the following year, in

Burnley, 1972

The successful promotion winning team pictured at Gawthorpe at the start of the 1972-3 season.

January, before they lost their second! What a season that was, losing only four league games in the entire 42 match season. And Keith played in every game – majestic, masterful, Keith Newton. He even scored in a most memorable and rather rare 3-0 victory at Villa Park. Over the years, was there ever a bigger graveyard of Clarets hopes than Villa Park? But not this time!

And so the Clarets won the league and promotion. With Docherty and Newton at the back, was it any wonder that Burnley only conceded 35 goals all season, the best defensive record in the country, and to this day, the second best record in the history of the club.(Second only to 1946-47 – what else?) Keith Newton played in 76 consecutive league games before being injured (Curiously, in the first game he missed, v Stoke away, the Clarets suffered their biggest league defeat for two seasons – 4-0!)

He was amazingly resilient, considering the hard manner in which he played the game. No games missed in his first season, three in his second, three in his third, one in his fourth, and by now in 1976, Keith was 35 years old. His partners came and went. Mick

Docherty was injured and Peter Noble played right back. Billy Ingham was tried and then Ian Brennan was introduced. Ian played left back so to accommodate him, Keith moved over to play equally as well at right back. Derek Scott came in at right back, even Brian Flynn was tried at full back, "The Doc" returned in 1975, and then Brennan, Ingham and Scott all took their turn again. But always, No. 3 Newton! It wasn't really until 1977-78 that the club felt the need to replace the old war horse. Keith Newton played his last game for the Clarets in February 1978, aged 36.

By the time he left Turf Moor in 1978, Keith had totalled more than 250 games for Burnley, proving to be surely one of the best buys ever for the Clarets (he came on a free transfer!) Anyone who ever had the privilege to see Keith Newton will retain a lasting memory of a truly great footballing Claret.

Peter NOBLE

1973-78

Midfielder
241 league games
63 goals

PETER NOBLE

Very few of us at Turf Moor had heard much of Peter Noble before December 1968. That was in the season, 1968-69, when though the Clarets were on the slippery slopes of Division One, the club were doing very nicely in the League Cup. Having beaten Grimsby, Workington, Leicester and Crystal Palace, all fairly comfortably, the Semi Final draw paired us with lowly Third Division Swindon Town. It could have been a lot worse – we could have played either Arsenal or Spurs!

However, things couldn't have got much worse! Against all the odds, Swindon came to Turf Moor and won 2-1! But the Clarets turned the table in the second leg and won 2-1 at Swindon. Came the Semi Final replay at the Hawthorns, and it seemed as if Swindon were about to upset the odds when they went ahead after nine minutes. But in the very last minute, David Thomas equalised to take the game into extra time.In the first minute of extra time, Frank Casper seemed to administer the final blow when he put the Clarets ahead 2-1. But it was not to be Wembley for Burnley, as first of all Arthur Bellamy put through his own goal to level the scores, and then very late on, someone called Peter Noble scored the winner for Swindon. (Swindon went on to beat Arsenal in the Final!)

Anyway, as to this"someone called Peter Noble"? Five years later, he arrived at Turf Moor – to stay! It was the summer of 1973, and the Clarets were on a high having just returned to Division One. Many felt that the team could hardly be improved, but Jimmy Adamson obviously knew better and Peter Noble was signed from Swindon for £40,000. He was a versatile player, which was maybe the main reason why Burnley signed him, and he had proved this at Swindon by being equally happy at half back or forward. He began as a substitute in the home game against Sheffield United, when the team read; Stevenson; Docherty, Newton; Dobson, Waldron, Thomson; Nulty, Casper, Fletcher, Collins and James. Substitute, Noble. In the game, Mick Docherty was injured and our new signing, half back/forward, Peter Noble came on as right back!

He was a major success from the start, and Peter played for the rest of that season as regular right back.The times, they were a-changing in 1974, with the departure of Martin Dobson, and it was in this season that we saw Peter's sheer versatility. He played in 46 games, occupying six different positions – right back, right wing, right half, left back, left half and even a few games at centre forward! With his move forward, the goals started coming. Though he played most of his games in defence or midfield, Peter finished third top scorer with 14 goals, including two against Tottenham and a hat-trick against his old club, Newcastle. He was non-stop, forever going forward, full of energy and enthusiasm, and from the start a real favourite with the Turf Moor crowd.

He was forever wherever the action was, and naturally,the goals began to flow. Quick to fasten onto the ball and a natural with his head, Peter Noble scored nine goals within seven games at the start of 1975-76. This spell included a hat-trick against Middlesbrough

Peter Noble, 1973-78

Peter takes to the air with this flying header against Spurs at Turf Moor in 1974.

and all four in the 4-4 draw against Norwich at Turf Moor. (Just imagine, scoring four goals and still not winning! A Turf Moor record?) Despite these goals, the Clarets were relegated from Division One that season. One of the problems was that Peter was injured and missed seventeen league games. The Clarets were relegated by two points and is there anyone who doubts that with Peter in our ranks, those two points would have easily been won. Sorry Peter, we're not blaming you!

Now back in Division Two, Peter Noble settled in at what was felt to be his best position – midfield. As if to make up for the games he missed in 75-76, Peter only missed three games over the next three seasons, and he truly became the general of the team. In 1977, he replaced Keith Newton as club captain, and the following season, he led the Clarets to victory in the Anglo-Scottish Cup – beating Preston, Blackpool, Blackburn, Glasgow Celtic, Mansfield, and Oldham Athletic on the way. He was inspirational and a born leader, and though he never led the club back to its position in Division One, when he left the club in 1979 the team went on a disastrous run of 16 consecutive games without a win, and were rightly relegated to

Division Three! By the time he left Turf Moor in January 1980 for Blackpool, Peter Noble had established himself as a fine captain, and a half back of great merit with a flair for scoring quality goals. He was the club's top scorer in 1976-77 and 1978-79 (both seasons playing midfield) and he is reputed never to have missed a penalty for the club. But most of all, Peter Noble won the affection and the hearts of the Turf Moor fans in the 1970's. He ranks with the best remembered players who ever played for our beloved Clarets.

Brian O'NEILL

1961-70

Midfielder
231 league games
22 goals

BRIAN O'NEILL

I'll admit it – we tend to be a rather nostalgic lot here at Turf Moor! Put that down to a few things – the successes we have had in the past or our seeming lack of success for so many years – but as I said myself a few years ago (in the 80's!): "We may not have much of a present, and we may have no future, but by gum, we've had a past!" And in a variety of ways, each week we celebrate the past, as sometimes we grimly hold on to our present – the Jimmy McIlroy stand, the Billy Watson bar, the Jerry Dawson bar, etc.

And when it comes to remembering our former heroes, few are as fondly remembered or as warmly welcomed when he returns, as Brian O'Neill, "The Bedlington Terrier." Brian came to Turf Moor for the first time as a 16 year old in 1959. He was one of the later arrivals from the North East following in the line of Cummings, Adamson, Angus, Robson, Pointer, etc, etc..

As a teenager, Brian was a member of the truly classic Reserve team at Turf Moor which won the Central League title twice, as well as the Lancashire Senior Cup. Players of the calibre of Irvine, Morgan, Lochhead, Bellamy, Towers, Meredith, Walker, Fenton, Thomson, Talbut and Joyce, were young Brian's colleagues in those fondly remembered days. Next to little Johnny Price, Brian O'Neil must have been one of the team's smallest players at 5' 7", but in contrast there was nothing diminutive about his commitment, his courage or his aggression. He never stopped – a veritable dynamo who tackled feverishly and was constantly in the thick of it, whether the "thick" meant the action or the mud!

He made his first team debut towards the end of the tumultuous 1962-63 season, whilst the club and the town were still shaking after the transfer of Jimmy McIlroy. The date was 30 April 1963, and the game at Turf Moor was against West Brom. The Burnley team that day read: Blacklaw; Angus, Elder; O'Neill, Talbut, Miller; Connelly, Robson, Lochhead, Simpson and Harris. Early in the following season, club captain Jimmy Adamson was injured and Brian, then aged just 19, came into the side to stay. His authority belied his years and he soon stamped his seal on every ground and game on and in which he played.

For the next seven seasons, Brian was a Burnley regular and a Turf Moor favourite. Whatever the club's fortunes, Brian O'Neill could be counted upon to be there in the midst of it – tearing into a tackle, driving the team up field, and inspiring the others to further heights, with his non-stop, all action style. Brian played in some famous games and helped to win some famous victories. Such as the last game of his first full season, against Spurs, a team of all stars which had won the FA Cup twice, achieved the double, and not been out of the top four for the previous five seasons. They were given their heaviest defeat for many seasons, 7-2, by the rampant Burnley side – with no player more rampant than the young O'Neill who scored twice himself that memorable day.

Such was the depth of the Burnley squad in those days, regularly fielding five teams each week, that other half backs of the quality of Dave Walker, Sammy Todd and David Merrington were contesting the number four jersey, but Brian O'Neill more than held his place in the midst of such sterling players. In 1964-65, though the Clarets finished in the bottom half of Division One for the first time in 13 seasons, they were still able to pull off some more than competent performances – like winning 4-2 at Blackpool, winning 4-1 at

Burnley, 1969

This was going to be, according to manager Jimmy Adamson, "The Team of the Seventies". Sadly, it was not to be.

Blackburn, and registering wins at home against Fulham 4-0, Sheffield Wednesday 4-1 and once again, reserving the best till last, hammering Chelsea in the final game 6-2. Brian O'Neill played in them all.

Following in the steps of Dave McKay (Spurs) and Jimmy Scoular (Newcastle), every team had an aggressive half back – (Leeds had at least two – Bremner and Hunter!), and the Clarets equivalent was Brian O'Neill, who could match any in the land for assertiveness and aggression. The Selectors took note, and Brian played for the Football League and the England Under 23's team. He was very much a part of the Burnley side which competed in the European Fairs Cup in 1966-67, being sent off against Stuttgart, scoring against Lausanne, and being involved in the "Battle of Naples", before going out to Eintracht Frankfurt in Round Four.

Brian could be relied upon to score some important goals, like the ones in 1967-68 against Stoke, Liverpool, Manchester United, Southampton and Leeds. But for those valuable goals and points won in those games, the club would surely have been relegated that season.(An absolutely unconsidered possibility in 1968!) But the writing was on the wall for the Turf Moor club, despite the team having such talent in its ranks as Ralph Coates, Dave Thomas and Brian O'Neil. Against increasing odds the club battled to survive in Division One. What defence the team had in 1968 was dominated by Brian O'Neil, who scored a memorable goal in the closing minutes to give Burnley the points against Manchester United,1-0.

At the start of 1969-70, Keith McNee in the *"Burnley Express"* said:"It won't be easy, but the Clarets can win the fight for survival." His words summed up the general atmosphere in Burnley; survival, rather than success. By now the big city clubs were totally dominating English football. In the previous 10 seasons, only two non-city teams had reached the FA Cup Final – Preston and Burnley. Whilst in the League, over the previous eight seasons, only one town team in the entire country had intruded upon the city club's domination of the top four teams in Division One – BURNLEY! They had been the only town team to have reached such exalted heights when they achieved third position in 1963 AND 1966! Now, you younger fans, can you begin to see the quality of the club that you and I so proudly support? I only wish that like me, my dad and my grandad, you too could have shared in such glorious days! Instead of like my own son, having to live on the memories of we"old-timers"! When we lived in Bournemouth, my son Christian was once asked who was his favourite player, and he very quickly and proudly answered:"Jimmy McIlroy, sir"(If some of us had had our way, the "sir would have preceded the name!) The class fell silent as they turned and looked at this Northern immigrant! "Surely, you mean Sammy McIlroy, don't you?" enquired the teacher."No sir" proudly replied Christian – "Jimmy McIlroy from Burnley!" (And Christian had never seen him play, nor even till then met the man.) That's what makes you a Claret!

However, I digress! In the season of 1969-70, in their fight for survival, the club having recently won the FA Youth Cup, turned to youth for the first team, and towards Christmas 1969, they fielded their youngest ever team in the First Division; Mellor (22), Nulty (20), Latcham (26), Docherty (19), Merrington (24), O'Neil (25), Coates (23), Thomas (19), Murray (21), Dobson (21) and Kindon (18). Within three years, seven of those players had left Turf Moor, presumably to find better things? One of the exodus was Brian O'Neil who was signed by Southampton in the summer of 1970. To secure his sought after signature, Southampton broke their transfer record and paid £75,000 for our young hero.

In his time at Turf Moor, Brian O'Neill had played in some 277 games and scored 25 goals.It was inevitable, in the eyes of many Burnley fans, that the following season, 1970-71, after his departure, Burnley suffered their first relegation to the Second Division for forty seasons! And to this day, many supporters still feel his loss. Such was the effect that this likeable young"Geordie"had upon us at Turf Moor – our beloved"Bedlington terrier"!

Louis PAGE

1925-32

Left winger
248 league games
111 goals

LOUIS PAGE

My dad, like his dad before him, liked wingers. My grandad had revelled in Billy Nesbitt and Eddie Mosscrop, whilst my father grew up admiring the skills of Jackie Bruton and Louis Page. Maybe this was all down to where he stood – pre-war on the old Longside,near the Bee Hole End. Later when I came on the scene, my dad promoted himself(and me!) to the old Enclosure,Bee Hole End. So we saw a lot of right wingers close up – Jackie Chew, Billy Gray, John Connelly and later Willie Morgan. But always, dad enjoyed any wingers, especially the fast variety like Elliott and Pilkington.

I suppose the tradition was begun for him by Bruton and Page in the 1920's. Though we've all had our favourites over the years, maybe Burnley have never had a better pair than these two. Both true Clarets. Both crowd favourites. Both English internationals.

Louis, who was born in Liverpool, came to Turf Moor in 1925, from Northampton Town. He was 25, and he had a growing reputation as a free scoring forward. He was to become a household name in Burnley. 1925-26 was an important year in the history of football, the season when the offside rule was changed. Because of this, Burnley who were on the slide (so what's new?) let in a lot of goals. A lot! 10 in the first game! 25 inside the first month! Five against West Brom, six against Manchester United, Blackburn, and Sheffield United, eight against Manchester City and Bury, 10 against (you wouldn't want to know!). And in the midst of this defensive chaos, Louis Page made his debut on the left wing (actually it was the first day of the season, when they let in ten against Aston Villa!) The team that fateful day read: Dawson; McCluggage, Waterfield; Basnett, Hill, Parkin; Kelly, Freeman, Roberts, Beel and Page.

The Clarets who only five years earlier had broken many of the league's records in winnng the League title, now found themselves in a season long struggle against relegation.Despite this lack of success, Louis was a revelation on the left wing and he was soon the top scorer. But with just nine games to play, Burnley were bottom. West Brom came to Turf Moor and won 4-3, Manchester City came and they too won, 2-1. Prospects were now bleak. Bottom with only seven games to play.

The last game that Easter was away to Birmingham, and the Clarets announced six team changes in the side to play at St.Andrew's. Dawson was dropped and in came Tommy Hampson; Fred Blinkhorn was brought in at right back for George Waterfield; Jackie Bruton came in on the right in place of James Tonner, who was moved onto the left wing; George Beel and Tom Roberts were dropped and Benny Cross and Louis Page took their positions in the middle. Louis Page, very much at home on the left wing didn't want the centre forward position, but he was persuaded to play, very much against his will. He remarked casually before the game,"I'll get six and stop at that!".

"PAGE THE PROPHET!" ran the headlines after the game, for that afternoon, Louis created football history, by scoring three in each half. Briggs the Birmingham centre forward was injured for the best part of the game, and this disorganised the home team completely. Benny Cross was the complete schemer and he reduced the Birmingham defence to shreds. Besides scoring a hat-trick before halftime. Louis Page also hit the bar twice. Then after Jackie Bruton had made it 4-0, Page scored three goals in little over three minutes!

The game was won 7-1 and those six goals remain as the club's individual scoring record to this day. If they hadn't have won that game, Burnley would have been relegated! As it was, Louis Page relaunched the rescue attempt and his nine goals in the last five games brought the club safety by a single point!

Incidentally, that season, Louis Page was the club's leading scorer, beating established strikers like Tom Roberts and George Beel. His 26 goals was by far the best to that day for a Burnley winger. And despite the valiant efforts of Messrs.Connelly, Kindon, James & Co in more recent years, Louis's 26 goals in a season is still a record for a Clarets winger.

Things were a bit brighter at Turf Moor the following season, 1926-27, and thanks to players like George Beel and Louis Page, the club finished fifth in the league. Louis scored two in the 5-1 trouncing of Rovers at Blackburn, and he had a run where he scored in four consecutive matches during December. His great talents were his speed and his shooting.If we had to compare him with any latterday Claret, it would have to be John Connelly. Like Connelly, Louis Page would often cut in from the wing to test the goalkeeper with some tremendous shooting. Typical of the Page talents is this newspaper comment from the Leicester v Burnley game in 1926-27: "Not a Burnley man seemed to be near. But at that moment, Page made a sudden rush, covering thirty yards in practically no time, and just as Campbell caught the ball, Page bundled him and the ball into the back of the net."It wouldn't have been a goal today, but it was in 1926 alright!

In 1927, Louis was chosen for England and altogether he won seven caps; he also later played for the Football League. The rest of Louis Page's career at Turf Moor was spent in annual struggles against relegation (finishing 19th for two seasons before going down in 1930) Louis was by no means to blame for this slide, as he played and scored, like no winger before or since. At the same time, George Beel was scoring his record number of goals, thanks almost entirely to the wing play of Bruton and Page who would sweep down both wings and swing across highly dangerous centres. For a winger, Louis Page was an incredible goal-scorer with annual totals of 26, 15, 22, 19, 15 and 13 goals, altogether 115 goals in 259 appearances.Just to compare left wingers, Brian Pilkington scored 77 in 340 games, Leighton James scored 81 in 397 games, and Steve Kindon scored 58 in 212 games; and they were all quite notable goalscorers. But not in Louis' league!

Sadly, due to falling gates and subsequent lack of finance, the club were compelled to sell Jackie Bruton, and without him the club were relegated in 1930. Gates of 40,000 in 1920 had dropped to 4,000 in 1930. Now in the Second Division (and struggling!), all the good players left one by one – Peter O'Dowd, Andy McCluggage, George Beel, and with the club next to the bottom in Division Two, Louis Page, the great Turf Moor favourite was transferred to Manchester United for £1,000. Sad, sad days.

My dad idolised him; I only ever saw Louis Page once.It was 1948 and I can still remember Dad being excited that Burnley were drawn against Swindon Town in the Cup, just a year since the Clarets had been at Wembley. Louis Page was the Swindon manager, and much to my dad's pleasure, that day he was sat just behind us in the Brunshaw Road stand (that was what managers did in the 1940's!). That was the day when giant killers Swindon knocked Cup Finalists Burnley out of the Cup, 2-0. But that day, my dad was far more excited at having seen his old hero, Louis Page, than he was about the Claret's stumble. Because he knew the sort of player that Louis Page had been for Burnley. A true legend!

Andy PAYTON

1998-2002

Forward
115 league games
68 goals

ANDY PAYTON

Paul Barnes was a more than decent centre forward. Burnley paid a club record of £350,000 to bring him from Birmingham City and he scored 30 goals in the 63 league games that he played for the Clarets. And many supporters were a little perplexed at his leaving the club in January 1998, in an exchange deal with Huddersfield Town for Andy Payton. Not that Andy was any slouch himself when it came to scoring goals; he had scored over 130 league goals for his previous clubs, Hull, Middlesbrough, Celtic, Barnsley and Huddersfield. (Indeed, he had already scored twice in games against the Clarets!) But on top of his feats and prowess came the important fact for a Clarets fan, that Andy Payton came from the town. He was to begin with a Burnley fan. And it showed from day one!

Day one was 17 January 1998 in the away game at Bristol Rovers, when the Burnley team read: Beresford; Brass, Winstanley, Harrison, Moore, Little, Waddle, Ford, Payton, Smith and Matthew. Burnley lost the game 1-0, and though Andy didn't score he hit the post! I think that it can honestly be said that the signing of Andy Payton alongside the introduction of Glen Little were factors which helped to turn the club around that season. It has been said that Andy Payton was a local hero from the moment he signed for the club; and there he stayed, held high in the esteem of the Turf Moor faithful. Andy was a mirror in which many Clarets fans saw themselves; a Burnley fan going onto the pitch at Turf Moor and scoring the vital goals.

And he was doing this within a week of his Clarets debut when he scored his first goal in the home game against Southend. But in some ways, we are racing ahead in the story. Andy was a Burnley fan as a youngster and signed schoolboy forms for the club when he was 14. However, he was allowed to leave the club when he was 16, and as Arthur Bellamy later said: "We made a mistake". And not for the only time in this collection, we must ask "What if? "What if Andy Payton had been kept on at 16 at Turf Moor?" Most certainly our club's history would have been different!

It was a crucial time for Burnley when Andy arrived at Turf Moor. The club were bottom of Division Two and looking racing certainties for relegation. Chris Waddle was the new manager, and some have said that it was the one positive action that he made all season in signing Andy Payton.

Wycombe	31 pts
Southend	27
Brentford	27
Carlisle	26
Plymouth	25
Burnley	24

The fight back began in January and Andy led the revival with five

Andy Payton, 1998-2002
Andy shows usual his combative side to his game – going in where it hurts!

goals in five games. By the end of the season, Andy had won four games with his single goal. But it all still needed to be done in the last match at home against Plymouth. With one game to play, despite Burnley's post-Payton revival, the league read:-

Brentford	50 pts
Plymouth	49
Burnley	49
Carlisle	44
Southend	43

The last match still had to be won. And it was 2-1. Burnley were safe. The crowd invaded the pitch, and later reflected on how almost single-handed 30 year old Andy Payton had scored nine goals in 19 games, and kept the dream alive.

The next season was much more of the same, except there wasn't a season long struggle against relegation. In many ways, the club was different now. The club had a new chairman, Barry Kilby and a new manager Stan Ternent. And the Burnley fans got used to seeing

Andy's goals. He was always it seemed in the right place at the right time, and 19 goals came that season from the "Padiham Predator" as he became known. Some were individual efforts – lobs, shots, headers, tap ins and flick ons, even penalties, whilst most came from the work of colleagues like Andy Cooke and Glen Little. Many were quite memorable such as his 35 yard lob over the keeper's head in the away game at Blackpool. But 1998-99 was just the start!

The new season of 1999-2000 began well with 10 points in the first four games and three goals from Andy! Before September was out, he had scored his first Clarets hat-trick against Colchester, a header, a shot and a penalty! That win put them top of the table for the only time that season. His second hat-trick came in the last game of 1999 against Oxford United. The Clarets won the game 3-2 and Andy Payton appropriately scored the final goal of the Millenium at Turf Moor. That put the Clarets in fifth position.

He scored five goals in three games in January as the Clarets maintained their promotion bid. But somehow, they couldn't quite catch up with league leaders, Bristol Rovers, Preston, Gillingham and Wigan. Ian Wright arrived at Turf Moor the next month, but even he couldn't overshadow "Payts". Andy scored his 20th goal of the season in the 1-0 victory over Wrexham, which kept them in fifth place as the end of the season closed in.

With four games to play, the Clarets were still fifth. And amazing to recall, they won all four and won promotion on the final day of the season. In doing so, they overhauled Gillingham, Millwall, Wigan and Stoke within the final fortnight. Andy Payton finished the season with 27 league goals, which won him the Golden Boot award. He was the highest scorer for the Clarets since Willie Irvine, some 35 years earlier! And this from a team which had fought off relegation two seasons before!

Burnley were back in Division One, but somehow the bubble had burst for local hero Andy. Despite his popularity with the Turf Moor crowd, he missed six games during the new season and he was announced as substitute on 21 occasions. New faces had been introduced to the club like Ian Moore and Gareth Taylor, and for some reason, as yet undisclosed, Andy became almost a sideshow for the main event on the pitch. On at least three occasions that I can recall, he came off the subs bench to score the winning goal! Cooke, Gray, Lee, Branch, Moore and Taylor all competed with Andy for the striker's role. Even Micky Mellon and Glen Little played up front with Andy sat watching!

That was the season when Andy, ever the man to set targets announced that he wanted to score a 100 goals for his native club at Turf Moor. At the start of 2000-01, it seemed a mere formality, but in his 18 outings he only had the chance to score nine goals. The following season was even worse, with just 15 games played and four goals scored. And before the season was ended, Andy had gone. First to Blackpool on loan and finally into what seemed to some, a hurried retirement.

Just five short seasons at Turf Moor – 81 goals! He could surely have reached his target just given the chance? Brave, quick and strong, he was a clinical finisher. And how the Turf Moor crowd loved this "Natural Born Claret". Any average football club is lucky to have a striker like Andy Payton just once every 10 seasons. Here at Burnley, we should count ourselves very lucky! Very lucky indeed!

Walter PLACE *(senior)*

1886-1900

Half back
136 league games
7 goals

WALTER PLACE (Senior)

My football education began at the home of my grandparents on Hollingreave Road. My dad was away in the War, and my grandad would educate me in all matters regarding Turf Moor. If my dad first took me to Turf Moor, then it was my grandad who first told me of the place and the club. If there had been an 11 plus concerning Burnley football, I would have passed it aged 5! We all have had our heroes, and if mine was Jimmy McIlroy, and my dad idolised Bob Kelly, Jackie Bruton and Louis Page, so my grandad used to tell me of James Crabtree, Jack Hillman, and Walter Place.(Even before I could count upto 10! First things, first! And like a good Claret, I too was telling my son Christian about Jimmy McIlroy before my son could walk!)

But to get back to Walter Place – he was without question the best known person living in Burnley for the last decade of the 19th Century. Burnley born and bred, Walter first officially appeared in the first team as a 16 year old in 1886-87 (pre-League days) The game was against Astley Bridge and it was an FA Cup Tie. The Burnley team read: McConnell; Whittaker, Birnie; Keenan, McFetteridge, Smith; McCrae, Place, Friel, Sugg, and Howarth. Burnley. ("The Turfites" drew 3-3 with Walter Place scoring twice) No doubt that he had played many games prior to this Cup Tie, but most of them went unrecorded.

Afterwards, he spent time at Colne and Bacup before returning to Turf Moor in 1890. In those early days, most towns and villages had their own teams and clubs like Astley Bridge, Read, Great Harwood, Clitheroe and Kirkham were among Lancashire's leading teams. So it was by no means a step down for Walter to go to Colne. Even Padiham could trounce Burnley in those days!

The first League game in which Walter Place played was against Wolves, away, on 1 November 1890. It was the club's third League season, and they were struggling! The team read: Kaye;Duerden, Walker; McFetteridge, Spiers, Keenan: Haresnape, McLardie, Lambie, Stewart and Place. In those early days of football, players were swapped and switched around from one position to another for each game. Because of this Walter was invaluable, he could play anywhere – and he did! His favourite position was right half, but he could play in any of the forward positions too. Twice in 1893-94 he even kept goal in place of the injured Hillman, against Blackburn and Everton.

It was a different world and game altogether from anything we experience today. Fights often broke out during games, such as during the Rovers-Burnley game in 1892. The same thing had happened the year before at Ewood when the entire Rovers team had walked off and claimed the match! Walter played in both of these games. By 1894-95, the club were gathering quite a few big names in their ranks – English internationals like Jack Hillman and James Crabtree, and Irish international "Ching" Morrison. Walter

Place was their colleague and contemporary. However, by 1895, the stars had left the club and players like Walter Place were left to try and keep the club together. This he did, with a struggle, which resulted in the club being relegated for the first time in 1897. As the club went down, Walter was an ever present, playing 35 competitive games that season. These included the four Test matches, where the top teams in Division Two played the bottom teams in Division One, an early form of the Play Offs we now have. Burnley only won one of the four games and went down! Faithful to the end, Walter played on in Division Two, turning out in four positions in 97-88 (nine games), the club's promotion year and 13 games in 1898-99, and a further 20 matches in the forward line as the 20th Century dawned.

But we have still only told less than half the story. Not only was Walter an all round footballer, but he was also a famous all round sportsman. He would compete at any sport, and do it well. He was one of the fastest sprinters in Burnley and he specialised in running backwards too! He was a roller skater, a snooker player, and a fine swimmer. He was a champion marksman with the rifle, he played cricket for Burnley and he was a leading local bowler. Few people could match him at any of these sports. He bred and flew pigeons and often won in competitions at that too. But he was maybe best known off the football pitch, for his exploits in the wrestling ring! In 1904, he fought the Russian champion Hackenshmidt and won, and gained the reputation of being the best wrestler in England. My grandad was still talking about this in the 1940's, when he first told me of Walter Place.

Walter had a younger cousin, also called Walter Place. Throughout the town, they were known as "Big Walter" and "Little Walter". They both played well over 150 games each for the club, and often played in the same team. Few players were as famous in their day, or as respected locally in retirement as Walter Place. People, like my grandad, Joseph Wiseman were delighted to tell their children and their grandchildren half a century later of the exploits of "Big Walter". A Burnley man through and through!

Ray POINTER

1957-65

Centre forward
223 league games
118 goals

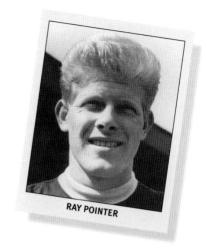

RAY POINTER

As the 1950's drew to a close, one of the main requirements at Turf Moor was a quality centre forward. The club had been well served by Billy Holden and briefly by Peter McKay, but since then we had seen Les Shannon, Ian Lawson, Alan Shackleton and later Jimmy Robson. None of these had been the sort of centre forward that the club desired, and none maintained the role. When Ray Pointer made his appearance in 1957, it seemed as if he was just another reserve being tried out. To begin with, Ray didn't strike the eye, despite his blond hair. He was in and out of the first team, scoring two goals in his first six games, four in his next 11 games and two in his next five matches. In between times, there were monthly periods when Messrs. Shackleton and Robson took over for a while.

Ray Pointer had first arrived at Turf Moor straight off the North East conveyor belt, which served the Club so well in the 50's and 60's. He made his first team debut in the week before his 21st birthday, in the away game at Luton, (5 October 1957), when the Burnley team read: Blacklaw; Angus, Winton; Seith, Adamson, Shannon; Newlands, Robson, Pointer, Cheesebrough, Pilkington. At first, there seemed nothing remarkable about the blond haired centre forward – he ran, he chased, he was keen, but nothing out of the ordinary. And this seemed to go on for some time.

But gradually he changed into something out of the ordinary. What caused the change? I don't know. Maybe, he was simply adjusting to the team and the pace? But to begin with, Ray was ordinary.And before our eyes, he became extraordinary! Some players have made Turf Moor worth attending, even in the darkest days.They alone have been worth the entry fee."Jimmy Mac"was one such player, Ralph Coates another. Peter Noble another. We could include Glen Little on song as another. Only a handful in my lifetime. But Ray Pointer must always be included in such a refined list.

We have had dozens of memorable players over the years, but Ray would stand out in any company. Certainly, the best centre forward in my lifetime to play in the claret jersey. My grandad would certainly name Bert Freeman. My dad would have chosen George Beel or Tommy Lawton. My son would opt for Andy Payton. But for me, it has to be Ray Pointer every time.No-one ever ran like him – not only the head down style, but the sheer amount of running. He chased the impossible ball, the 50-50 ball with the goalkeeper, the opponent dallying or dithering with the ball, or the through ball from McIlroy or Adamson.There was never a lost cause where Ray Pointer was concerned, and that was what made him so watchable. Times without number, he has scored from impossible situations, in which any other forward would have given up the chance or the chase.

He was more than competent with his head too, and the style of play in the 1960's encouraged him to lurk around the opposing area. Not for him "total football", where you often see the striker back defending a corner. Certainly, total commitment, which involved him in difficult and sometimes even dangerous situations. I am reminded of the Burnley v Manchester City game in October 1959."Then came the alarming Pointer incident. He and McTavish chased a long pass and disputed possession wide of the goal on the dead-ball line. Pointer trying to turn at speed, crashed into the boundary wall onto the back of his neck. Dr.Iven and Ray Bennion rushed round, and ambulance men were on the scene with a stretcher. However, doctor and trainer half-carried him between them towards the dressing room. It looked a permanent retirement for Pointer, but to everyone's astonishment, he came out again after a few minutes, and played better than before!" *(Burnley Express)* Such was Ray!

In his first full season in the first team, 1958-59, Ray scored 29 goals, a post war record for the club.The team scored 81 goals between them, another Burnley post-war record. The football was beginning to flow and goals were beginning to come, such as Turf Moor had never seen for over 30 years. On eight occasions, Ray

Pointer scored a couple – and these included away games at Manchester United, Newcastle, West Brom and Preston. The club finished in the top seven clubs for the fourth season running, but more and better was to come.

What happened in 1959-60 is part of football history in general and Turf Moor history in particular.For his part, Ray played his role in winning the League title with a further 23 goals, including two against Preston (away), against Wolves and Notts Forest, as well as a couple against Bradford City in the FA Cup.The League title was won, and rarely can a

Ray Pointer, 1957-65

Ray posing proudly for the camera in his England shirt.

young centre forward have had such a start in league football – 52 goals and the title within two seasons! And there's more!

Ray's scoring powers and his influence on the Burnley team grew each season. In 1960-61 (European Cup year), Ray scored another 26 goals, with two against Fulham, Wolves, Bolton (away), and a hat-trick against Arsenal (away!) In one magical sequence, he scored ten goals in six consecutive matches! The *"Burnley Express"* said of him: "One continues to be amazed at the non-stop, full speed chasing by Pointer, the retriever of lost causes, and the taker of unexpected half-chances."

The story goes on. In 1961-62, Burnley scored a hundred league goals for the second season running, and of this century, Ray Pointer amassed a further 26 goals (two against Bolton, West Brom, Everton, and Birmingham, as well as in the away game at Spurs. He also recorded a hat-trick in the 6-2 away win at Birmingham City.) Being present at three quarters of these games, it is highly tempting for me here to wander off into memory land , but those Clarets fans under 30 years of age just wouldn't believe me anyway! Forgive me for recalling my favourite month of all time – September 1961, when the

Clarets played seven and won the lot! (Four were away from home!) There was an amazing spell when the team won three away games in the space of a fortnight, Birmingham 6-2, Leicester 6-2, and Fulham 5-3. And Ray notched up nine goals himself that month! Forgive the golden memories of an old Claret, but I don't know of any players like Ray Pointer these days.

Let the last word on the 1961-62 season come from the Leicester City programme for the Semi Final replay, Burnley v Fulham, April 1962:

"THIS WAS SOMETHING TO REMEMBER"

"With all deference to the gallant Fulham, the regular Filbert Street patrons remember vividly the brilliant exhibition by Burnley, when they won here 6-2 on 20 September. Leicester's football would have been too smart for the majority of sides, but Burnley's fast, smooth rhythm proved irresistible. Few will dispute the contention that no better blend of speed, grace and power, had been forthcoming at this ground in post-war football."

Because of the arrival of Andy Lochhead on the Turf Moor scene, Ray Pointer moved over to the inside right spot in 1962-63, and maybe this was the reason for his reduced number of goals – just 14 that season. Although a far better reason was the departure of "Jimmy Mac" with half the season to play. By this time, Ray Pointer was a regular international player, as of course were half the Burnley first team! Sadly, late in the season, Ray was badly injured in the game at Nottingham Forest, and from then on, his appearances in the first team were rare and infrequent.

Indeed, except for an occasional game, it was a full nine months, before we saw Ray back in the first team. Sadly it was only for 10 league games in 1963-64 and a further three in 1964-65, before Ray Pointer left the Turf Moor scene as a first team and first class player. In August 1965, Ray moved on to Bury for a nominal £8,000. He later played for several other clubs,scoring many more goals, but never in the proportion that he did during his Turf Moor days. Like the majority of Burnley players who moved on to other clubs, we saw the best of him during his days in claret and blue.

He left us having scored 133 goals for the club, the second highest total in the club's history. His unquenchable spirit and the non-stop running made Ray Pointer one of the most popular players ever at Burnley. I've been with him on a few occasions since, on youth pitches at Blackpool and on the occasion of my 50th Birthday party, and he's always a delight to be with. Our thanks and appreciation of Burnley fans everywhere are due to the unstoppable Ray Pointer.

Alick
ROBINSON

1933-39

Wing half
204 league games
8 goals

ALICK ROBINSON

My father used to call them "the forgotten years". He was referring to the thirties at Turf Moor, when Burnley were fairly in the doldrums. It was pre-war, sandwiched for Clarets fans in our memories between the glory days of the 20's and the heady heights of the 40's and 50's. Dad liked to go on a bit about some of the "great" footballers that Burnley had in those days, players often overlooked and forgotten by today's generation of supporters. I would smile at his golden memories.

But on reflection, dad was right. There were some great players then – truly great, though you might have to search for a while. Players came and went like nobody's business in the 1930's. Dozens of players were signed, as the club struggled near the foot of Division Two. During the summer of 1932, rumours swept the town that the Football Club would not carry on in 1932-33. However, the fears were dispelled by the Board of Directors at a special Jubilee Meeting held at the Mechanics Institute in July.

In 1933, well over 20 players were signed – not all of them got into the first team. Ten players were tried as centre forward – Mays, Mantle, Beel, Bowsher, Drinnan, Kelly, Jennings, Page, Edwards and Cecil Smith. (We used to stand next to Cecil in the 1950's when he stood in the Enclosure!) But from the dozens of players whom he saw in the thirties, dad used to tell me of players like Tommy Gardner, Billy Miller, and most of all Alick Robinson .

Alick came from Bury in 1933 for nearly £5,000 (a sizeable fee in the 1930's) It was a record fee for the Turf Moor club to pay, but he proved to be good value in the coming years. He played first at Brentford on 7 October 1933, when a much changed Burnley team looked like: Scott; Richmond, Waterfield; Brown, Bellis, Robinson; Sellars, Hancock, Smith, Douglas, Miller.

Alick was a left half, a grafter, with great passing skills. His arrival certainly steadied the ship, because after finishing 19th for the previous two seasons (and escaping relegation on both occasions by two points!), the club managed a respectable thirteenth in Alick's first season. They never again struggled against relegation during Alick Robinson's time with the club. Inside a month, Alick had been appointed team captain, a wise move. Later that season, the Clarets were drawn against Alick's previous club, Bury in the Cup, and 37,379 turned up to see the game. (The average gate hadn't topped 15,000 for the previous five seasons!) As well as playing regularly at left half, Alick also made appearances at left back, right half and outside left in his first season. He was an invaluable asset.

1934-35 saw Burnley win five and draw one in their first seven games. This put Burnley in the strange position of being amongst the Second Division leaders. Perhaps as a result of these successes, Alick Robinson was chosen to play for the English League against the Irish League, alongside numerous established First Division stars. The half back line read Cliff Britton (Everton), Sam Cowan (Manchester City) and Alick Robinson(Burnley), which shows the recognised class of the Burnley's captain. Though the team later faded in the league table, they did manage a Cup run, reaching the Semi Final, where they were beaten by Sheffield Wednesday. The great game in 1934-35, still recalled by those who were there, was the Sixth Round Cup Tie against First Division Birmingham City, when Burnley, admirably led by Alick Robinson came back to win 3-2 after being two goals down

There was very little interest in professional football in Burnley in the mid thirties. Crowds came for the big Cup occasions, but for the bread and butter of the League, attendances were often appalling. In 1935, the lowest gate for 24 years was recorded at the Burnley v Norwich game (2,800), though three hours later, 3,333 saw the

Hospital Cup semi final at Turf Moor! Curiously in 1934-35, the team turned out wearing blue jerseys with claret sleeves!

They changed again in 1935-36 to white shirts with black shorts and white stripes. That was the season that Tommy Lawton arrived in the first team, and on his first game against Doncaster Rovers, the Burnley team was: Adams; Richmond,Hubbick; Hindmarsh, Johnson, and Robinson; Hancock, Brocklebank, Lawton, Hornby and Fletcher, quite a different team from two years previously when Alick had first arrived.

In 1936-37, the Cup saw Burnley drawn at home against the Arsenal. Arsenal were very much the outstanding team in the country at that period, having won the First Division four times in five seasons; they were also the current Cup holders, so it is easy to imagine the excitement that the draw brought to Burnley. There was talk of the club's record attendance being broken, and one reporter described the game as the greatest match ever to take place at Turf Moor. However, the record attendance was not broken, the 54,445 were just 330 short, but the gate receipts of £4,025 were a new record for the club. The teams on that historic day were: Burnley; Adams; Richmond and Hubbick; Rayner, Wood and Robinson (captain); Stein, Toll, Richardson, Brocklebank and Fletcher. Whilst Arsenal were: Boulton; Hapgood and Male;Crayston, Roberts and Copping; Kirchen, Bowden, Drake, James (capt) and Bastin.(Phew, what a team!)

I was brought up with the memories of my dad about that game. He always swore that a "goal" which Bob Brocklebank "scored" after ten minutes was a genuine effort. The referee disagreed with my father and the vast Burnley crowd, and said that the ball did not cross the line, and when the ball was cleared by the Arsenal defence, he waved play on. What might have happened if that goal had been allowed, no-one will ever know. What did happen is now history, and my father and the other 54,444 people present never forgot it. The Arsenal team ran riot, with Ted Drake getting a hat-trick in the first 20 minutes and they left Turf Moor,7-1 victors. Kirchen on the right wing was described in the *"Burnley Express"* as "the fastest thing on two legs that has ever been on Turf Moor" and the newspaper commented that Arsenal just gave up trying when the score reached six! However, Alick Robinson held his head high, and the money made from that Cup Tie and the Lawton transfer made all the difference in the club's future. By 1938, Alick Robinson was one of the most respected half backs in the land. He continued to be club captain and during 1937, '38 and '39, he played at right back, as consistent and reliable as ever. On 2 September 1939, Burnley played at Birmingham and fielded the following team: Adams; Robinson (capt), Marshall; Gardner, Woodruff, Bray; Hays, Brocklebank, Clayton, Dryden and Hornby. The following day, war was declared and the 1939-40 football season was technically over. That day saw the end of many players careers and it was the final league game for Alick Robinson.

Though he played in 100 games for Burnley during the war, by the time hostilities ceased, Alick was 40 years old.and he called it a day. Alick Robinson was without question the outstanding Burnley player in the 1930's. He helped the team recover from the doldrums of relegation and he saw the seeds sown for the assault on the Division Two title in 1946-47. "Forgotten years" indeed, but Alick Robinson is far from being a forgotten Claret!

Jimmy ROSS

1897-99

Forward
29 league games
51 goals

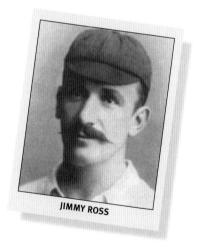

JIMMY ROSS

Jimmy Ross was a legend and a national hero even before he came to Burnley. He was a Scot and he had come to Preston in 1884, four years before the Football League began. He scored eight goals in the famous 26-0 victory of Preston over Hyde United in 1887. He must have been among the first players in the country to play 100 league games, and ditto, concerning 100 league goals. Such was his success, that it would be interesting to discover if he was the first League player to play 200 games (with Preston and Liverpool) and later 300 games in the Football League (with Preston, Liverpool, Burnley and Manchester City)?

In this humble collection, I haven't dwelt too much anywhere on pre Burnley days or post Burnley days for any player. But, it's important to glance at some of Jimmy's exploits, prior to his arrival at Turf Moor. He was the George Best of the Victorian era, attracting great crowds wherever he played for Preston. With him in their side, Preston won the double in 1888-89 and the League Championship for a second time the following season. The team were known as "The Invincibles". He was known as "King James" or "James 1" and he was one of the very first dribblers of the ball. All those who came afterwards, from Stanley Matthews to Glen Little have followed in his tricky footsteps.

The first time he came into Burnley's history was on the first day of the Football League on 8 September 1888, when Preston North End were at home to Burnley in their first league match – Preston won 5-2 and Jimmy Ross scored twice. Nine years later, Jimmy came to Turf Moor, via Liverpool. It was March 1897, and sadly the great man arrived just too late, as the club experienced relegation for the first time. The day that Jimmy Ross first played for Burnley was away against his former club, Liverpool, and Burnley won 2-1 against the team who finished fifth in the league. The Burnley team read: Haddow; Reynolds, McLintock; Place (Sr), Brown, Taylor; McVean, Ross, Toman, Place (Jr), Ferguson. His arrival equalled anything we have seen in recent years with the arrival of Ian Wright or Paul Gascoigne, and the team that had played in front of gates of three and four thousand, had over ten thousand at Turf Moor for their last two games, as they were relegated.

The following season was an entirely different story. With Jimmy Ross in their ranks, the "Turfites" were unstoppable. They played the first eight games in Division Two without defeat, Ross scoring five times in the first six games. By the end of the season, they had won 20 of their 30 games, and they'd only lost twice in the league. The goals came like never before and never again, and over the year they recorded victories over Blackpool 5-1, Wolves 5-0, Grimsby 6-0, Kilmarnock 6-0, Nelson 7-3, Newton Heath 6-3, and Loughborough 9-3. Of course, they weren't all League games, but it must have been great stuff to watch! Jimmy Ross played in 27 of the thirty league games and he scored 23 goals. In doing this, he broke Tom Nicol's club record of 17 goals, and set up a target which lasted ten years before it was broken by Dick Smith.

Particularly effective was the manner in which Jimmy teamed up with centre forward Wilf Toman, as the club recorded their first League title, albeit in the Second Division. However, all was not well in the Turf Moor camp, and the following season, the town hero,"King James" fell out with his Irish team-mate, right winger Tommy "Ching" Morrison. As a result, Jimmy was transferred to Manchester City, where he was to play a major part in their success alongside Billy Meredith and Burnley's own, Jack Hillman. We are left with yet another of those cases of "what might have been?" After Jimmy Ross left Burnley, the club dropped nine points in their last ten games, and still only finished six points behind the League Champions. What if…?

But in any history of association football, the name of Jimmy Ross will always stand alongside the all-time greats of the Victorian era. And for two years and 63 games,"King James" reigned at Turf Moor.

Len SMELT

1919-25

Full back
229 league games

LEN SMELT

My grandad would gaze into the fire and discuss aloud with himself who were some of the greatest players he saw. At full back, was it Bamford and Taylor or Smelt and Jones or Smelt and Taylor? He, (I think, looking back I was a mere 8 year old!), opted for Smelt and Taylor. He certainly talked a lot about Len Smelt. Just a name to me, but for grandad a host of memories.

Len came into my grandad's life in March 1919, when he was transferred from Gainsborough Trinity. (the same club from which Burnley had previously signed Sewell, Gunton and Jones, the entire Gainsborough defence in 1913.) Len's first game of the 1919-20 season, the day that league football resumed after the war, was away to Notts County, when the Burnley team read: Dawson; Smelt, Jones; Taylor(W), Boyle, Watson; Kelly, Lindsay, Freeman, Norris and Mosscrop. William Taylor and Patrick Norris may soon have disappeared from the scene, but the others will still surely be spoken of in Burnley in a hundred years from now!

The club had won the FA Cup in 1914 and finished fourth in the League in 1915. Great things were expected by the people of Burnley and they were not to be disappointed! Nevertheless, eyebrows and voices were raised in protest when admission prices at Turf Moor were increased. The admission to Stand A went up from 1s 3d to 2s; the Enclosure increased from 8d to 1s, whilst entry to the Ground was 9d.

From the start, Len Smelt proved a great success at right back. He was the only ever-present in the team that season, as the club finished in second place, their highest ever final position in Division One, He had a series of left back partners – Cliff Jones, Harry Hastie, George Halley and in the end after a long illness, the old favourite of the Turf Moor crowd, Dave Taylor. But with them all, always Len!

In those far off days, full backs had to be hard men, and Len was such a player. Strong, difficult to beat, always reliable, Len came to be as much a part of the Burnley team as "Halley, Boyle'n Watson" themselves! He rarely missed a game – only four in his first four seasons at Turf Moor, and those were all missed through illness. On reflection, I can see the way that my grandad thought. Len was never a member of the Cup winning team in 1914, but he was an indispensable part of the even greater team which won the League Championship in 1921.

Except for his illness covering three games, he played in the rest of the famous 30 consecutive league games without defeat. As in 1919-20, his partners at left back came and went – Taylor, Jones, Lindsay, Astin, Halley, later Pearson and Evans, and later still, Wheelhouse and Fergus, before George Waterfield arrived on the scene in 1924-25. "Outstanding" was a word often used in the local press to describe a Len Smelt performance. Such was the comment in the "Burnley Express" after the 1-1 draw at Bolton in 1921, when 54,809 broke the Burnden Park record.

He made his 100th consecutive appearance for the first team in 1923-24, when he played against West Ham, but in contrast to Billy Watson who had accomplished the feat in 1913, the club was refused permission to present Len with a suitable memento. Later that season, Len played in the historic FA Cup Tie against Huddersfield Town, when the attendance record for Turf Moor was established. The team that day read: Dawson; Smelt, Taylor; Bassnett, Hill, Morgan; Emerson, Kelly, Beel, Cross and Weaver. Len was injured in the game and so came to an end his 117 consecutive appearances for the first team. During his later absence, Burnley only won one game in the last eight matches that season, and escaped relegation by just four points.

By 1925, Len was now 40 and he played his final game for Burnley at Arsenal on 18 April 1925. He had proved to be a wonderful servant for the Turf Moor club, and thousands of my grandad's contemporaries must have agreed with Joseph Wiseman that Len Smelt was as good as they come.

Trevor STEVEN

1981-83

Midfield
74 league games
11 goals

TREVOR STEVEN

Over the years, Burnley Football Club has been famous for a number of things, but maybe most of all, for its Youth policy whereby so much young talent has been developed. It all began in the late 1930's with the introduction of youngsters like Tommy Lawton, Fred Taylor and Harry Potts, and some might say, it's final discovery in the 1980's was

Trevor Steven. And its finest? Trevor came from Berwick upon Tweed and he arrived at Turf Moor, aged 16 in the summer of 1980. Even so young, he stood out from the crowd as an exciting prospect, and it was little over a year later that he made his first team debut, still aged only 17. The game was away to Bristol Rovers (September 1981), and the Burnley team read: Stevenson; Laws, Holt, Scott, Overson; Dobson, Cavener, Taylor, Hamilton, Steven and Potts. Though the Clarets went down 2-1, Trevor Steven's performance displayed so much maturity and authority that his first team place was practically guaranteed for the future.

And so it was that young Trevor, still only 18, played through the 1981-82 season, starting at number 10, but soon moving over to number 8 in the right midfield. It was not an easy time to make a debut at Turf Moor. Burnley were in the Third Division and were struggling. In their first eight games that season, they won just once. They were now well established in the bottom six clubs in Division Three. But with the likes of past, present and future internationals like Mike Phelan, Martin Dobson, Trevor Steven and Billy Hamilton in the team, success simply had to come. And it did.

Starting with a 2-1 victory at Portsmouth, the Clarets played from early October to mid March without losing a League game, (twenty games in all).It was surely more than co-incidence that this was the time that the Burnley crowd witnessed the emergence of Trevor Steven as a major force. He was a truly exciting youngster to watch from the terraces, and the Burnley crowd were quick to appreciate that something very special was taking shape"before their very eyes" (in the words of Arthur Askey!) His first goal came in November 1981, in the away game Reading, when his 30 yard shot simply flew into the net.

But it was not only the Turf Moor faithful who were taking notice of the new young talent in their midst,; the nation was beginning to sit up and pay attention to this raw young talent, who really was anything but raw. His ball control allied to his passing and distribution skills made some of the older generation recall the young Martin Dobson in the 1970's and even the great"Jimmy Mac" of the 1950's. So it was then when still only 18, Trevor made his debut for the England Youth squad, when he played against Scotland in March 1982.

With the continued success of the first team, the club found

Burnley, 1982

themselves heading for the top. And a further sequence of seventeen games with only one defeat brought them the Third Division title and secured promotion. Trevor was very much at the heart of that fine team achievement, and the Turf Moor faithful knew that here was a youngster with a future. Accompanying such a triumph, the crowds began to return to Turf Moor, and on the last match of the season against Chesterfield, 18,711 attended, the highest gate for four seasons.

It really had been a bottom to top season, as the team rose from the bottom six to take the title, but it was not half as topsy-turvy as what followed in the 1982-83 season which followed. "Burnley were back" in Division Two, where we felt we belonged(!), and now we were just one step from regaining our "rightful" place in Division One, where we had been only six years previously. But life proved to be much harder in the Second Division than anyone, management, players or fans, had imagined.

After a reasonably good start with two wins and a draw, success deserted the team. One game was won in October, just one in November and not even one in December, when the team lost all five games! By Christmas, the team were bottom, and the struggle continued against relegation to the season's end. Unsuccessfully. There was a mini revival with four wins in the New Year, but another five successive defeats in March and April put paid to any escape. You could hardly blame Trevor Steven. Indeed the youngster played his heart out in 54 games that season (a League record for an 18 year old?)

The reason for so many games was that alongside Burnley's slide back into Division Three, the club had two remarkable Cup runs, in both the FA Cup and the League Cup. During those cup runs, Burnley beat the likes of First Division teams such as Coventry City, (away) Birmingham (home) and Tottenham (away). What a game that last one was and what a night for the faithful Burnley fans, as the Clarets went wild, winning 4-1 against the current FA Cup holders and League Cup Finalists. Against all the odds, the Clarets achieved one of the unlikeliest and most improbable wins in their history, with young Trevor more than matching the Argentinian star Ossie Ardiles.

And many of we Clarets fans thought we might have done even better in both competitions but for two strokes of ill fortune. One was for Steve Taylor to miss a penalty in the F.A. Cup Quarter Final at Turf Moor against Sheffield Wednesday(!*?!*! … I could say more!) We lost the replay at Hillsborough. And the other bad luck was to be drawn against Liverpool in the League Cup Semi Final. Despite missing a few chances, the Clarets didn't stand much of a chance at Anfield against a Liverpool team who won the Division One title for the second year running and went on to win the League Cup at Wembley. But through all of these adventures, there was young Trevor Steven in the thick of it, playing against world class players and more than matching their skills.

It was impossible to believe that Trevor Steven for all his loyalty to Burnley would stay at Turf Moor to face another season in Division Three, and so very soon after the arrival of John Bond as club manager in 1983, Trevor was sold to high flying Everton for £325,000. He went on to win so many trophies for his future clubs that we would need another page to list them all, plus three dozen England caps, with his transfer fees totalling nearly ten million pounds. Like so many other fine footballers, some of the finest this country has ever seen, we at Turf Moor were privileged to see such remarkable talents at an early age.

Whenever he is to be seen on TV as a soccer pundit, I smile and remind anyone in the room, that he was once a Claret! One of the world's stars – one of ours!

Dave
TAYLOR

1913-24

Full back
221 league games
5 goals

DAVE TAYLOR

David Taylor was one of the most popular full backs ever to play for Burnley. And he was certainly the fastest. Before becoming a professional footballer, Dave was an athlete, known all around Scotland for his sprinting. When he settled as a footballer, he had the reputation of being the fastest full back in the country.

There had been a problem at left back for some years at Turf Moor, and the fans had seen 11 players in that position, all within three seasons, 1908-11. Tom Bamford, Tom Splitt, Jim McLean, Harry Woodward, Roland Boden, Hugh Moffat, Bill Howarth, Alec Leake, Herbert Wilcox, Fred Barron, and Bob Reid, all took their turn before Dave Taylor appeared on the scene from Bradford City in December 1911.

He had won an FA Cup winners medal with Bradford just seven months earlier, and his signing was quite a coup for the Turf Moor directors. His arrival came at one of the most exciting times in Burnley's history, as the 1914 Cup Final team took shape. Freeman had arrived the previous season, Tommy Boyle just three months earlier, and the club were challenging for promotion for the first time in thirteen seasons. Dave Taylor's first game for the up and coming Turf Moor team was in the away game at Huddersfield, in December 1911, when the team read: Dawson; Reid, Taylor; McLaren, Boyle, Watson; Snowden, Lindley, Freeman, Hodgson and Harris.

However, after a season long race with Derby and Chelsea, the team from the banks of the Brun came third, just two points off promotion. But it was merely a foretaste of things to come. In 1912-

13, Burnley carried all before them in Division Two, as from November to January, they won eleven consecutive games, scoring forty goals against seven conceded. Indeed the surprise result on 25 January 1913 was Burnley 3 Nottm Forest 5 (at the time, Burnley were top and Forest next to the bottom!) It was Burnley's first home defeat since 20 March 1911, 22 months earlier.

By this time, Dave Taylor was well established in the Burnley defence. A strong player, hard tackling, his speed was legendary. He was so fast that he even scored the winner in the first game of the season against Glossop. Bob Reid had been the regular right back on the other wing, but in 1912-13, Dave began to be partnered by Tom Bamford, who had arrived from Darwen. The two gelled immediately, and the Bamford-Taylor partnership was born. Altogether, they were to play well over one hundred games as Burnley's full back pairing.

One of the games they played together was when Burnley beat Gainsborough Trinity 4-1 in the FA Cup in February. More sensational than the match itself was the sequel when Burnley caused a stir throughout the whole football world, by signing the entire Gainsborough defence, goalkeeper Sewell and full backs Gunton and Jones. Perhaps as big a sensation at Turf Moor itself was the fact that the following Saturday, the regular defence of Dawson, Bamford and Taylor were all "rested" as the three new signings all made their debut.

1913-14 was the season when the Burnley team made history by winning the FA Cup for the first time. Dave Taylor was an indispensable part of that team and the only games he missed were through injury. He also played in all eight FA Cup Ties including the memorable win in the Final at Crystal Palace. In the Third Round win against Bolton, the *"Burnley Gazette"* reported "Dawson did his job to perfection and Bamford and Taylor were towers of strength." Incidentally, it is a little known fact that the week before the Final, Burnley went to Manchester City and were trounced 4-1. Jerry Dawson collided with a City forward and was forced to retire with severe rib injuries. Dave Taylor went in goal for the rest of the game, and proved that he was a far better full back than goalkeeper!

Straight after the City game, Burnley set off for their training headquarters at Lytham, where they had stayed before every Cup Tie. They returned to Burnley on the day before the Final, and then embarked on the train at Bank Top station. They were given a great send off by hundreds of local people. The team was followed later in the day by 14 excursion trains which travelled down to London after work on Friday evening. Around 15,000 people (including my grandad!) were on those trains (return fare 12s!) and because so many of the town's working population were away, most mills closed down for the weekend.

But came the day itself, and Dave Taylor was a vital part of the team that won the FA Cup for the only time in the club's history, beating Liverpool 1-0. I've known that team since I was five years old! Sewell; Bamford, Taylor; Halley, Boyle and Watson; Nesbitt, Lindley, Freeman, Hodgson and Mosscrop. Their names roll off the tongue like poetry! Meanwhile, there had been a Reserve game at Turf Moor, where a board had been carried around at intervals giving the Crystal Palace news "NO SCORE". We can only imagine the great roar that spread round the ground as news of Bert Freeman's goal came through. The progress of the game was also relayed to the offices of the *"Lancashire Daily Post"* in St. James' Street, and throughout the afternoon, the town centre was so packed with people that the traffic had to be diverted. Thousands of people stayed out in the streets all that night celebrating the victory. The *"Burnley Express"* headline ran "BURNLEY'S CROWNING TRIUMPH" as the paper told how greatly the King had enjoyed the occasion.

Local schools and mills closed for the day on Monday. The train carrying the team arrived at Rose Grove station, where the players boarded a wagonette. From the station, the triumphant procession made its way into Burnley, down Accrington Road and on Trafalgar. When they turned the corner of Trafalgar into Manchester Road, a great crowd of well over 50,000 greeted them with a loud roar. And so it was that captain Tommy Boyle, sitting in his shirtsleeves at the front of the wagonette, sat next to Dave Taylor, brought the F.A. Cup back to Burnley. Within months, the country was at war with Germany.

After the War, Dave Taylor was seriously ill at home in Scotland for many months, and he didn't return to the town or the team until April 1920. But he never really settled back in the team, and after eleven games in the Championship season of 1920-21, he lost his place to Cliff Jones (one of the three transferred from Gainsborough in 1913.) However, after having only played 31 games in three seasons, in 1922-23 he found himself the first team choice again at left back, as Cliff Jones had left the club. Indeed, David Taylor only missed two games all season, as he and Len Smelt teamed up to make a partnership remembered for years afterwards. 1923-24 saw a similar story, as the pair totalled up over a hundred appearances together as a full back twosome.

After exactly 250 games in Burnley's colours, Dave Taylor, now aged 40, left Turf Moor to return to his native Scotland. Burnley have had some fine full backs in their time, but over eighty years after his final Turf Moor appearance, Dave Taylor still rates as one of the best. Once seen, never forgotten!

Dave THOMAS

1967-72

Winger
153 league games
19 goals

DAVE THOMAS

Every player spoken of in this humble collection has had his fans and followers over the years. But David Thomas lays claim to being one of Turf Moor's favourite sons. What is it about our memories that still brings a shiver of excitement when his name is mentioned? Why do some of the older generation still glow a bit when his name crops up?

Was it his youth? Because Dave Thomas was "nobbut" a lad of 15 when he first walked into Turf Moor. Before he was 16, he was chosen to play for England Schools against Northern Ireland Schools in April 1966, even before he ever played in the Reserves! Getting in the Burnley Reserve team was no easy option in the mid-60s, such was the quality of Burnley's young players; but Dave Thomas was obviously a talent on a different level from the norm. His natural ball control, his balance, his style of running (with flapping arms!) made him stand out on any pitch. He could (and would) take on opposing defenders with confidence, and his shooting power was obvious to players and fans alike..

Such talent shouted out to be tried in the first team, and Dave's time arrived in the last game of the 1966-67 season in the game against Everton. Regular left winger Ralph Coates was injured, and so the Burnley team lined up as follows: Thomson; Smith, Elder; Todd, Angus, Latcham; Morgan, Lochhead, Blant, Harris and Thomas.

It was 13 May 1967, and the Turf Moor crowd saw history being made. That day, young David was just 16 years and 220 days old. He was the youngest Burnley player ever to play in the First Division and the club's second youngest player of all time (second only to the legendary Lawton, 46 days his junior.)

The following season, 1967-68, saw Dave Thomas make just three first team appearances. He had wingers of the calibre of Morgan, Casper and Coates to contend with for a place in the first team (did we ever have such a dilemma?) But more than playing for the first team, Dave Thomas helped to create a little more Turf Moor history, by being a vital part of the Burnley Youth team which brought back the F.A. Youth Cup to Turf Moor for the first time. On the way to the Final, the young Clarets beat the youth teams of Manchester United, Manchester City, Sheffield United and Everton, which showed to future generations the strength of the class of '68 at Turf Moor. That team contained the likes of Mick Docherty, Alan West, Eric Probert, Steve Kindon and Dave Thomas, who between them went on to play a total of well over 1,500 Football League games for their various clubs. Three of the team were Youth Internationals, and two became England Under 23's players. And in 1967-68, they were all trying to get in the Reserve team at Burnley!

In the summer of 1968 Willie Morgan was transferred to Manchester United, the latest hero whom we saw grow up at Turf Moor, play for us and then leave the club. Such has always been the sad pattern for the Turf Moor faithful! But Morgan's departure left the door open for young Dave to establish himself in the first team, at the ripe old age of 17! And he seized the opportunity. By now, the much changed Burnley team read: Thomson; Angus, Latcham; O'Neill, Waldron, Merrington; Coates, Lochhead, Casper, Bellamy

Burnley, 1970

The team which was relegated for the first time in 40 years! The side lost more games that season (22) than in any other season in the club's history, and young Eric Probert (front row left) was top scorer with five goals! And this with the likes of Dobson, Thomas, Coates and Casper!

and Thomas. Soon, because of injuries to Bellamy and Angus, players like Dobson and Kindon came into the first team, making the team appear; Thomson; Smith,Latcham; Todd, Waldron, Blant; Thomas, Murray, Casper, Dobson and Kindon. With so many youngsters in the team, they were christened "the babes" and Colin Waldron became the youngest club captain in the country.

It was "take-off time" for the young Clarets team and in the Autumn of 1968, they raced to eight consecutive victories, scoring 22 whilst conceding only three goals. The highlight for the Burnley team on the pitch and the Clarets fans on the terraces was surely the 5-1 trouncing of Leeds United at Turf Moor. Leeds were the League Champions that season, and only lost two league games in the season, but that day, that glorious day, they met their match. And how! The Burnley team, playing with breathtaking pace (Coates, Kindon, etc.) and amazing skill (Thomas, Casper & Co.) were unstoppable, as the champions to be, left Turf Moor with their tail

Dave Thomas, 1967-72

Don Revie described Dave Thomas as "The finest talent in Britain".

between their legs! Such was the talent, with players like Dobson, Kindon and Thomas to the fore, that Jimmy Adamson later made his famous prophecy that Burnley would prove to be "The Team of the Seventies". It was not to be, but it would have been a very brave person who would have dared to challenge Jimmy Adamson's claim in 1969. By now, Dave was a member of the England Under 23's team (still only aged 19!) and prophecies concerning his future were beginning to be fulfilled. Jack Hixon, the legendary talent scout for Burnley in the North East had described the 15 year old Thomas as the finest prospect he had ever seen, whilst Leeds manager Don Revie said of the 17 year old that he was "the finest talent in Britain, and possibly the whole of Europe."

Towards Christmas 1969, the Clarets were fielding their youngest ever team in the First Division; Mellor (22); Nulty (20), Latcham (26); Docherty (19), Merrington (24), O'Neil (25); Coates (23), Thomas (19), Murray (21), Dobson (21) and Kindon (18). But the writing was on the wall, as the club which had started the decade as League Champions, finished the 1969-70 season in 14th position for the fourth consecutive season.

In 1970-71, the wheels came off! Burnley lost the first game 2-1 to Liverpool at Turf Moor, and the headline in the *"Burnley Express"* ran "GRIM START STUNS FANS", but events were going to get a lot grimmer. After seven games, the Clarets still hadn't won and Dave Thomas had scored the only goals (two) in those seven games. The team seemed to get younger with every match, and Dave Thomas at 20 years of age seemed like a veteran compared to the 17 year old Leighton James! Dave played and ran his heart out for Burnley that sad season, but to no avail. The Clarets ended up relegated for the first time since 1930, and I felt as sad that day as my dad had felt in 1930, and no doubt, my grandad had done in 1900!

Getting out of the Second Division proved a lot harder than the club anticipated, and the talented Thomas had his first taste of football at a lower level. It is amazing on reflection to think that we had stars like Waldron, Dobson, Thomas, Fletcher, Casper, Kindon & Co, and we still struggled. But 1972-73 was somehow different as the team hit form again. David Thomas scored three in the first five games, including a superb individual goal from over 20 yards to beat Preston, and three days later another Dave Thomas special helped to beat Portsmouth, away.

Behind the scenes, there were rumours of a rift between manager Adamson and young Dave, and matters came to a head when our young hero was transfer listed. Despite this, his appearances and goals still made him one of the great favourites with the Turf Moor crowd, now returning in their thousands. And so it was that in October 1972, with Burnley now top of Division Two, the troubled star left Turf Moor, to go to of all places, Queen's Park Rangers, who were by now among Burnley's main rivals for promotion. A reported £165,000 was paid for the multi-talented 21 year old, and many thousands of Burnley fans were sad to see their favourite player leave Turf Moor.

Now all that happened well over thirty years ago, and Dave Thomas went on to play several times for England in his later career. But we at Burnley were left with glorious memories of a golden boy – Dave Thomas racing down the wing, hair flying, arms waving, socks always around his ankles, Dave Thomas gathering the ball, teasing an opponent, before setting off towards goal, Dave Thomas on the ball, jinking right and left seemingly almost touching the ground as he leant sideways, Dave Thomas taking corners and free kicks (was there ever a better kicker of a dead ball in the last fifty years at Burnley?) Most Burnley folk would feel that he could have achieved more, especially if he had stayed at Burnley, but like the vast majority of those who have come and gone, I believe that we saw the best of Dave Thomas whilst he was at Burnley.

Always a pleasure to watch, the memory of such a young and gifted Claret have helped the likes of me get through many a struggling season since at Turf Moor. And his memory helps keep an old man warm on many a winter's night.

George WATERFIELD

1923-35

Full back
371 league games
5 goals

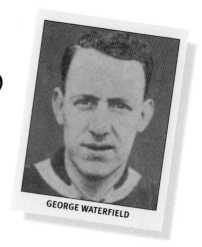

GEORGE WATERFIELD

As I have suggested before, great full backs (in my mind!) have usually come in pairs. Grandad told me times without number of Smelt and Taylor; I myself was weaned on Woodruff and Mather. But for my dad, it was always McCluggage and Waterfield. I grew up feeling them to be like my uncles!

George Waterfield was a classic left back and played for England in that position. Indeed, I suggest that he played longer in the left back position than anyone else has ever done at Turf Moor. But he started as a left winger. When he came to Burnley in October, 1923 from Mexborough Town, he was an out and out winger and that was where he made his League debut in the home game against Sheffield United. The Burnley team read: Dawson; Smelt, Taylor; Basnett, Hill, Watson; Bennie, Kelly, Beel, Cross and Waterfield. Burnley had paid just £450 for George and what a bargain that turned out to be!

He faced stiff competition for the left wing spot from established first teamer Walt Weaver, and in 1923-24 Walt won, 21 games to 17! The battle for the wing position continued until Christmas 1924, when with the score 11-9 in George's favour, George was switched to left back. It was the hardest game of the season against the team which would finish the season as League Champions, Huddersfield Town. The left back position was proving a problem since the retirement of stalwart Dave Taylor. Evans, Wheelhouse and Fergus had all been tried, without much success. The club had won only four times in twenty games and relegation threatened. And so George

Waterfield made his debut as a left back, partnering the veteran Len Smelt. The move proved so successful that George remained at left back and though the club finished in the bottom four, they escaped relegation.

In the summer of 1925, the club bought Andy McCluggage and the partnership of McCluggage and Waterfield was born. It was 29 August 1925 and it wasn't the best of days. That day was the first when the new offside rule was played, and Burnley (new full backs or not!) were walloped 10-0 by Aston Villa! Things didn't improve much after that, but stalwart play throughout the season by Andy and George ensured survival in Division One for another season (just!) And that was how it was from 1924 to 1930, struggle after struggle, until the club were finally relegated. In the meantime, Jack Hill, Jackie Bruton, Jerry Dawson, and Bob Kelly had all gone, but McCluggage and Waterfield played on. By the time Andy McCluggage left the club in 1931, the regular rearguard of McCluggage and Waterfield had played in 170 first team matches together. It was a club record for a full back duo until the days of John Angus and Alex Elder and they topped 270 games together!

But just think – 170 games spread over six seasons at Turf Moor. No wonder my dad thought the world of them; he saw them practically every week throughout his teenage years; they must have been like his closest friends! And when Andy left, still George played on at left back. In February 1927, he was chosen to play for England, such was his standing in the country as a full back (And remember these were the days of outstanding left backs like Sam Wadsworth and Ernie Blenkinsop.) In 1934-35, his twelfth season at Turf Moor, he became only the third Burnley player in the club's history to play 350 league games for the club.

George was a strong, hard player; you had to be in the tough football days of the twenties and thirties; he was a much respected player both at Turf Moor and much further afield. His name is synonymous with Turf Moor and to this day over seventy years after he left the club, he is high in the top twenty of all-time appearances for the club, finishing only six short of four hundred. I'd have been shot by my own father if I hadn't have included George Waterfield in this selection of vintage Clarets. Few people have served the club so faithfully.

Billy WATSON

1909-24

Half back
380 league games
18 goals

BILLY WATSON

There is something rather appropriate in the fact that this small effort on my part to remember some vintage Clarets of yesteryear should conclude with one of the all-time greats. There is even a Billy Watson bar at Turf Moor these days and only last Saturday, I glanced up at the name as I bought a coffee there. More than once, over the years, I have I heard people asking: "Who was Billy Watson?" And once again, I repeat that he was one of the all-time greats.

Five years before Jimmy McIlroy had heard of Burnley, I had heard of Billy Watson. My grandma used to talk of him, just as much as my grandad! That was how well known he was, particularly to that older generation in the town. I don't think my grandma ever went to Turf Moor, but she knew of Billy Watson. Everybody did!

"Halley, Boyle 'n' Watson!" True local legends. Heroes. Immortal figures in our small town. They won the Cup. They went 30 games without being beaten. They won the League title. They have gone down in local history as being part of perhaps the greatest of all Burnley teams. And the story of "Halley, Boyle 'n' Watson" begins at Turf Moor in March 1909 when Billy Watson arrived at the ground. He had been signed from his home town club of Southport Central, the same club that Eddie Mosscrop came from three years later.

Billy's first game in a Burnley jersey (green at the time) was just a month after he was signed on, in the away game at Chesterfield. The Burnley team read: Dawson; Barron, McLean; Watson, Leake, Moffat; Morley, Mayson, Smith, Abbott and Smethams. Burnley were then a struggling team in Division Two, finishing the season well into the bottom half. Of that team, just Dawson and Watson were to see the years of Burnley's greatest triumphs, whilst others like Lindley and Bamford were in the Reserves at the time.

It took a couple of seasons for Billy to find a regular place in the first team, but when he did, in October 1910, he was there to stay. Indeed, it was a very rare Burnley side for the next ten seasons that appeared without the name of Billy Watson. It must have been a very exciting time to follow the team, as my grandad did, in those pre-war days. The team was being strengthened each year, and grew into a team that challenged for promotion in 1912 and won promotion in 1913. No player was more central in the growth of that classic Burnley side than Billy Watson. He was an ever present(38 games) in the team that challenged for promotion; he played 32 games in the promotion season, and he never missed a game in the FA Cup run of 1913,which took the club through to the Semi Final.

By 1912, Billy had already played a hundred games for the first team. In October 1911, he had been joined by Tommy Boyle from Barnsley. But in March 1913, Burnley made one of their most significant signings of all time when they signed George Halley, a right half, from Bradford. This brought together George Halley, Tommy Boyle and Billy Watson as the Burnley half back line. They made their first appearance together in March 1913, when Burnley beat Bury 2-1 at Turf Moor. How many people who saw that game, realised that they were in at the beginning of a new era in the history of Burnley Football Club? That season, Billy Watson made his international debut for England, when he played against Scotland. Previous to the International match, he had made over a hundred consecutive appearances for Burnley, but unfortunately he was injured in the International match and missed most of the remaining games that season.

To celebrate the winning of promotion, Philip Morrell, the MP, gave a dinner at the Mechanics Institute in Burnley That evening, there was a presentation to Billy Watson, on the occasion of his playing 100 consecutive League games for Burnley. He was presented with a gold watch and chain, and a specially inscribed medal.

1913-14 was to prove the greatest year so far in the life of Billy Watson. In brief, he was a regular member of the First Division team, only missing games when he was chosen either for the Football

League or for the England team. He was an ever present in the same team that played seven cup ties in all, in winning through to the FA Cup Final. He was a vital member of the winning Cup Final team at Crystal Palace. He was one of the first players ever to receive a winners medal from the King himself. And triumphantly, he returned with the team and the Cup to Burnley to be received as local heroes. Top that! And he would, given time!

After the War, more honours came his way when he was chosen to play again for England against Wales. One national paper reported that "Watson was the pick of the English half backs", and immediately after the match, he was chosen again to play against Ireland. He certainly captured the headlines in 1919, because after his international appearance, he was chosen again, this time to play for the Football League. And then in November, he scored a spectacular goal in the game against Manchester United. Eddie Mosscrop put the ball into the penalty area, and it was headed out; then came Watson's 20 yard shot from outside the penalty area: "Who can recall Watson's goal, without at the same time remembering Watson's action as he thundered down the field with big hefty strides, uttering at the same time, his long drawn out cry of "Hey-up!" It was an action which in a manner, hypnotised the whole of the players, and they practically stood still, waiting for him to shoot. Nearly all the players stood transfixed watching the ball go into the net, having moved their heads more as an act of curiosity to see what the ball would do, more than anything else." (*Burnley News*, 15 November 1919)

Then in November 1919, Tommy Boyle returned from a lengthy injury, and "Halley, Boyle 'n' Watson" played together again for the first time for five years. That day, Burnley beat Bradford 1-0 at Bradford, and went to the top of Division One for the first time in their history. But in the end, after a mediocre period over Christmas, when the team went seven games without a win, the team finished the season as runners up to West Brom. Again, it was the first time that Burnley had finished runners up in Division One. Merely, the beginning!

Time and space forbids me to relate the wonders of the 1920-21 season, maybe the greatest season in 125 years of Burnley Football Club history. But Billy Watson played in every game, the only player in the club to do so.(62 games in League, FA Cup, and Lancashire

Burnley, 1913

This was the team which won promotion from Division Two. Players featured in this book are Billy Watson (back row left), next to him, Jerry Dawson, George Halley (back row next to right) and Bert Freeman (back row right). Captain Tommy Boyle is seated at the front with the ball, and full back Dave Taylor is seated front row, right.

Cup) The record books tell us that the team lost their first three games, against Bradford City twice, and Huddersfield. The record books go on to tell how the club then embarked on a record breaking thirty league games, from September to March, without losing a game. A record for Burnley in particular and football in general! What the record books don't tell is of the style of Burnley's League Championship winning season – great goals from "Joe Andy", the sheer brilliance of Bob Kelly and the dominance in match after match, of "Halley, Boyle 'n' Watson". The only hiccup in the season was when George Halley contracted pneumonia and missed the last sixteen games.

But the aim of the game was achieved and Burnley (now called "The Clarets"instead of their previous nickname"The Turfites") were League Champions for the first time in their history. Let the last word about the 30 games without defeat come from a man of the times,"Kestrel"who wrote all the Burnley F.C. articles in the *"Burnley News"*."So an end has been put to Burnley's record breaking run. But do we mind? Not a bit of it! We have been partners with the greatest team that ever was. We know full well that never in our time will such a thing be accomplished again, and we like to think that we live in an age that will be remembered, when we personally are forgotten." How true you were, Kestrel old friend!

The next season, the team finished third, slightly disappointing, but severely hampered by long periods of absence through injury by Halley, Boyle, Watson, Nesbitt and Cross. It was the end of a glorious decade summed up by the local paper. "The greatest regret of the season was the break up of the grand old line of half backs, Halley, Boyle and Watson." Their last game together had been the game against Blackburn Rovers on 11 February 1922. Despite their lasting fame, it is a curious fact that they only played 115 games together as a half back line; less than three complete seasons. Football legend, Billy Meredith said of them in 1921:"I doubt if one of those sound old plodders could do the hundred yards in 14 seconds. They use their brains more often than their feet." Whilst my uncle who watched them every week once wrote to me: "Do you want my opinion of that team? Don't say "No!" I'm bursting to give it! It was a good team, but not a great one, a well balanced team, better in its whole than in its parts. One super star, Bob Kelly, and a group of hard working, more than competent players, men who knew their business and played so very well together. Billy Watson, the classic example of a spoiler, played a good part of the time in a crouch and made a lot of his tackles from a sitting down position; George Halley, just the opposite, he played tall. After fifty years, I can still picture him, a beetle browed man with the ball at his feet, with all the time in the world, pushing the team forward. And Tommy Boyle, a great defensive player with a very good head – not just for getting his head to the ball, and in that he was amazing, I think it had something to do with timing. But he could be surrounded by much taller players, they would all go up for the ball, but Tommy's head was the one that connected – he always knew where the ball was going, and there he was in the thick of things."

By 1922-23, a much changed Burnley side appeared in the first game: Dawson; Smelt, Taylor; Emerson, Sims, Watson; Fisher, Kelly, Anderson, Cross and Mosscrop. Billy Watson was still there, the king pin of the Burnley defence. With his experience, he now played at right half too, occasionally at full back, and even once on the left wing. He was still in the first team in 1923-24, as the team began to slide slowly down the League table. And he made his final appearance for the Burnley team on 8 September 1924, when he played at Turf Moor against Everton. Curiously, by now, the last surviving members of the League Championship team were the two original players who saw it all begin to happen in 1909 – Dawson and Watson. By the end, Billy had played in 380 first team games over a period of 15 seasons. Not for the first time, we can only wonder at what he and the club might have achieved, but for the intervention of the First War.

The contribution by Billy Watson to Burnley F.C. and English football is best described by another football reporter of the day in the *"Lancashire Daily Post"* during 1924: "In passing review of the principal figures in the game during the last 14 or 15 years, I cannot recall one who stands out so distinctively as Burnley's left half back for consistent brilliance. It is a very rare thing indeed for Billy Watson to play even an indifferent game, or even rarer for him to be absent from his place in the side. I do not think he has exactly received adequate recognition from the authorities, because he is a more accomplished artist than any other left half of his time, equally good in defence and recovery, as in attack. He is cleverer than Grimsdell, less showy than Bromilow, more polished than Bobby McNeal, Sturgess, Utley, or any of those who have flattered for the moment and flashed in and out of the representative side. His virtue of quiet workmanship veils some of his real strength." That says it all!

A Final Word!

Whilst writing my various books on the Clarets, many people have asked whom I believe to be the best players of all. I have tried to suggest a few in this modest effort.

I will edge my bets and offer you six teams, who are in my humble view, the best of a tremendous bunch. Two pre-war. Two post-war (up to 1973) and two 1973 to the present day.

PRE WAR PROBABLES:
Dawson;
McCluggage and Waterfield:
Halley, Boyle and Watson;
Bruton, Kelly, Freeman, Cross and Page.

PRE-WAR POSSIBLES:
Hillman;
Smelt and Taylor;
Crabtree, Hill and Leake;
Nesbitt, Miller, Anderson, Beel and Mosscrop.

Not a bad choice for someone who never saw any of them play! I rely entirely on what my family saw and told me. And what about Alf Bassnett, Cecil Smith, Bob Brocklebank and Tommy Lawton? Well, I only had twenty two places!

And Post-War? Well, here's where I come into my own, because I've seen them all, and I can recall everyone of them like well loved friends.

POST WAR PROBABLES:
McDonald;
Angus and Elder:
Adamson, Cummings and Shannon;
Connelly, McIlroy, Pointer, Coates and Elliott.

POST WAR POSSIBLES:
Blacklaw;
Woodruff and Mather;
Attwell, Brown and Bray;
Morgan, Irvine, Lochhead, Thomas and Pilkington.

And you say, what about Peter McKay and Jimmy Robson and Billy Holden and…? O.K., O.K., I'll even give you a "Third Team":-

THIRD TEAM:
Strong;
Aird and Winton;
O'Neil, Waldron, and Miller;
Chew, Morris, Holden, Robson and Harris.

And of the "modern era?" Let's say since 1973, when I wrote the first edition of *"Up the Clarets!"* A few problems here, because the traditional positions have changed so much from 2-3-5 to 4-4-2 to 3-5-2 to 4-5-1, etc. What would Tommy Boyle have made of all that? So, just to bewilder the younger generation (for a change!), I'm sticking to the traditional positions of two defenders, three half-backs (midfielders) and five forwards (I know it takes some believing kids, but that's the way it used to be! And we used to score 100 goals in a season!!)

MODERN PROBABLES;
Stevenson;
Laws and Newton;
Noble, Dobson and Flynn;
Little, Casper, Hamilton, Kindon and James.
(What a forward line!)

MODERN POSSIBLES:
Beresford;
Hird and Brennan;
Phelan, Thomson and Davis;
Francis, Steven, Payton, Heath and Eyres.

And you say, what about Paul Fletcher, Ted McMinn, Mick

Docherty, etc,etc."Should I go on? There isn't enough time for me to speak of." *(Hebrews Chapter 11. V 32)* Go on, play the game yourself!

And having chosen those teams, I wonder which would win if they met? I can't help remembering what happened in 1883, when Burnley F.C. held a trial match, and the "Improbables" beat the "Probables", 8-3!

Rev. David Wiseman